how to do UPSIDE DOWN
FOR KIDS

HOW TO DRAW UPSIDE DOWN FOR KIDS

-How to Draw Books For Kids-
Using the Technique of Drawing on The Right Side of the Brain

How To Draw Upside Down For Kids
© Kamdon Kreations LLC.
October 2020

Published by:
Kamdon Kreations LLC.

All rights reserved. How to Draw Upside Down For Kids
is under copyright protection. No part of this journal may be
used or reproduced in any manner whatsoever without written
permission.

For inquiries contact: Kamdokreations@gmail.com

Illustrations © 2020 by Kamdon Callaway

ISBN -978-1-7355447-1-7

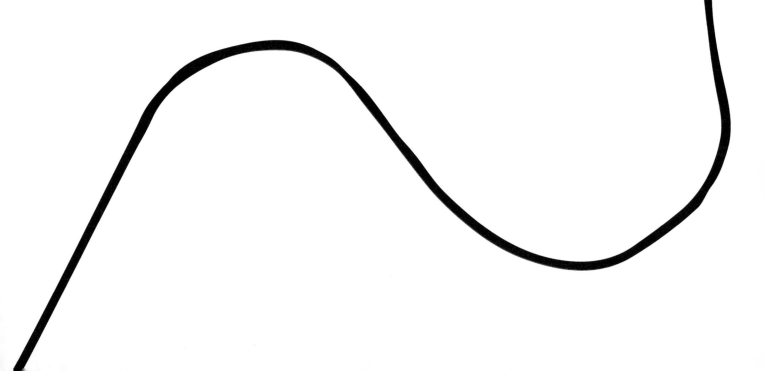

Illustrated By
KAMDON CALLAWAY

Kamdon Kreations LLC.

Pencil & Eraser

The awesome thing about drawing is that you can use tools laying around the
house. Try to find a good pencil, eraser and extra paper to start
your drawings. Start sketching with a light touch,
and then you can erase and add definition
when the base of your drawing is complete.
Most important thing is to practice and have fun!

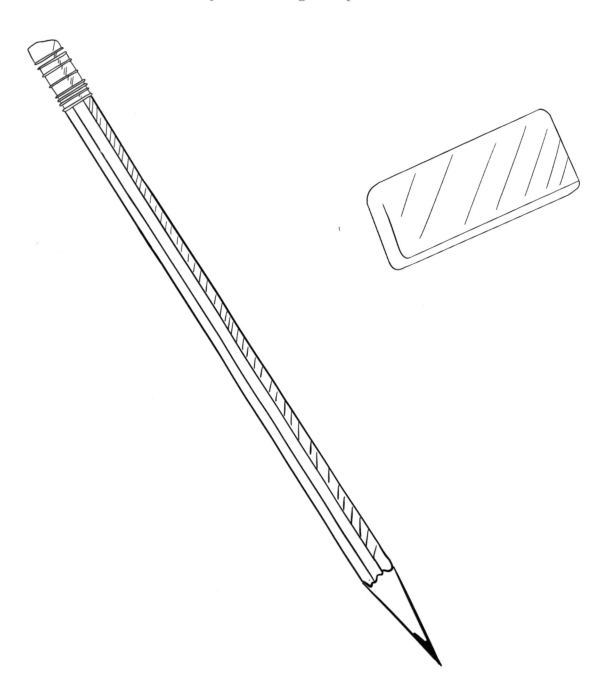

How to Steps

1
Start with basic shapes.
Circle
Oval
Square
Triangle
Lines.

2
Lightly draw each shape. Remember, the light lines are guide lines in the book. The dark lines are finishing touches.

3
Erase extra lines.

4
Go over all the edges to make a clear, crisp drawing.

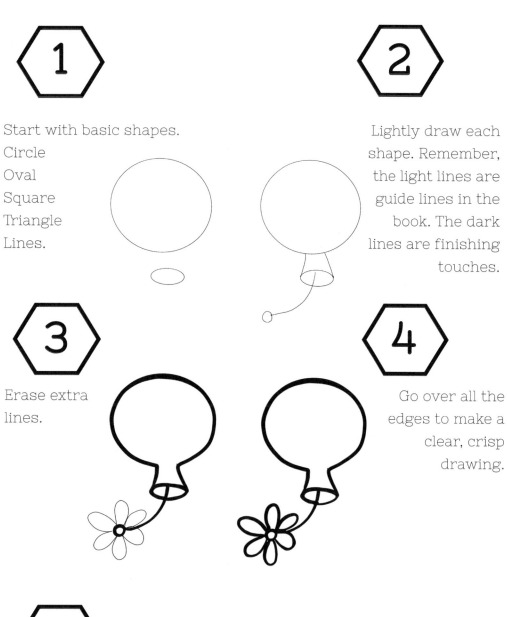

5

To see your masterpiece!

it's time

UPS
NM

to draw IDEOO

FLIP

FLIP

FLIP

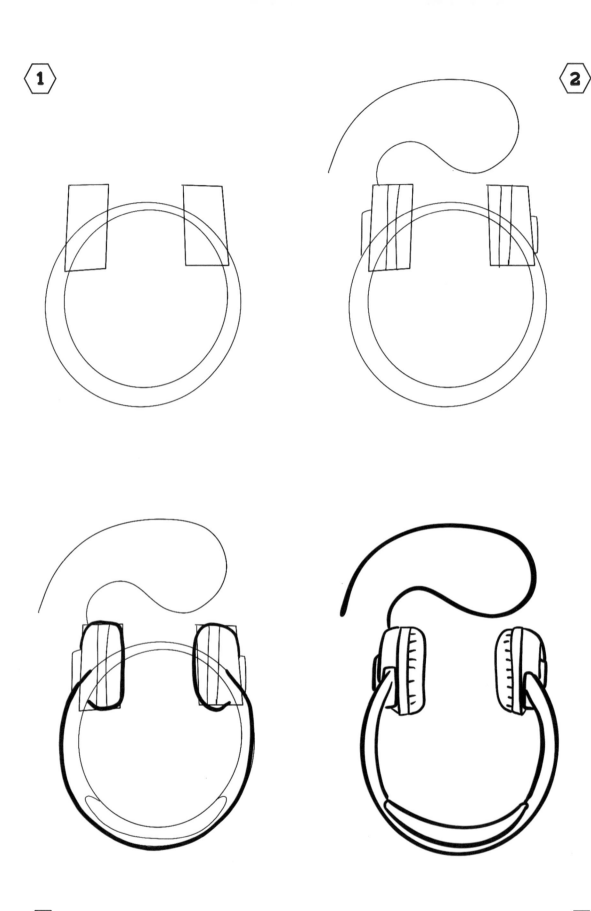

FLIP

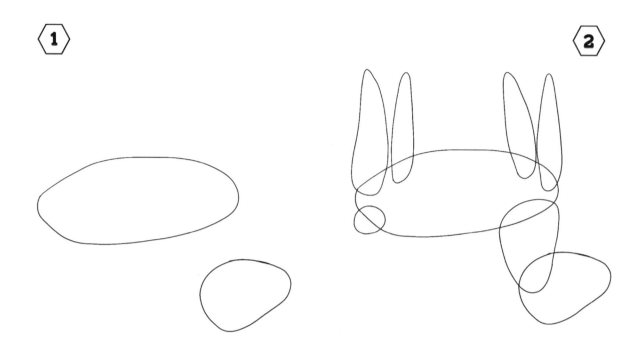
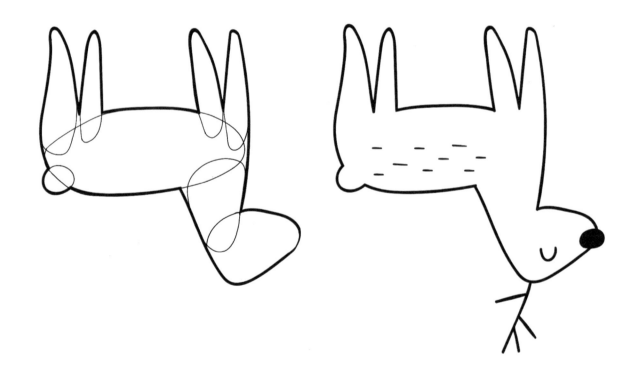

FLIP

FLIP

FLIP

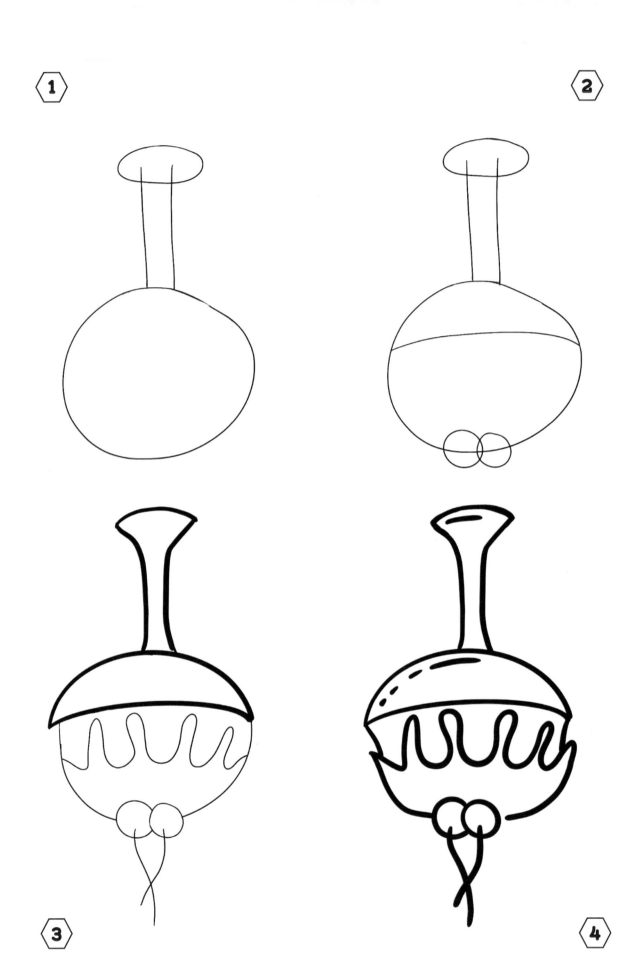

FLIP

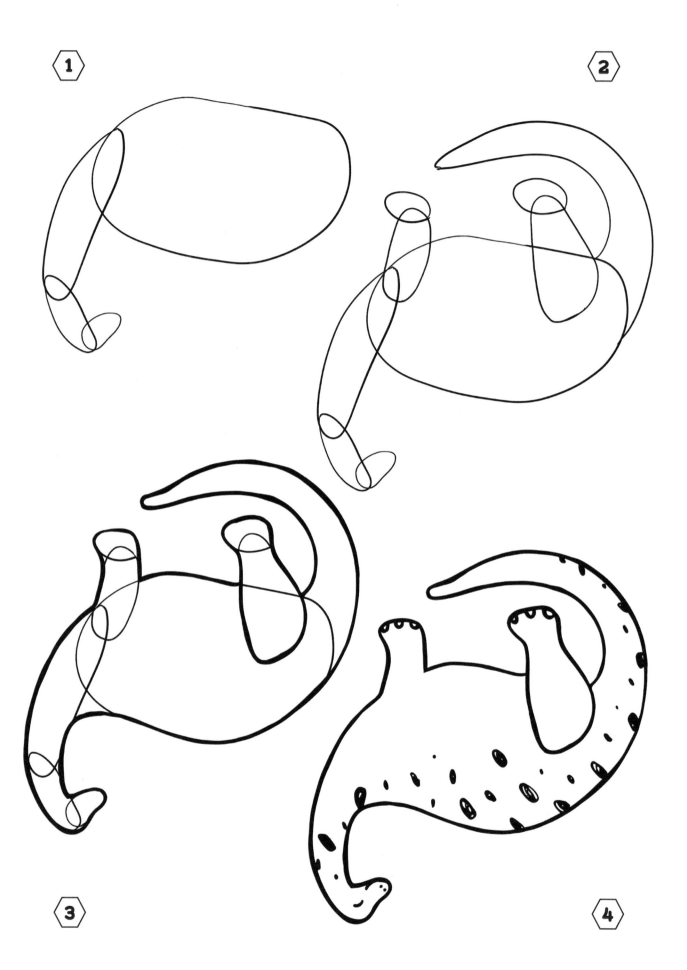

FLIP

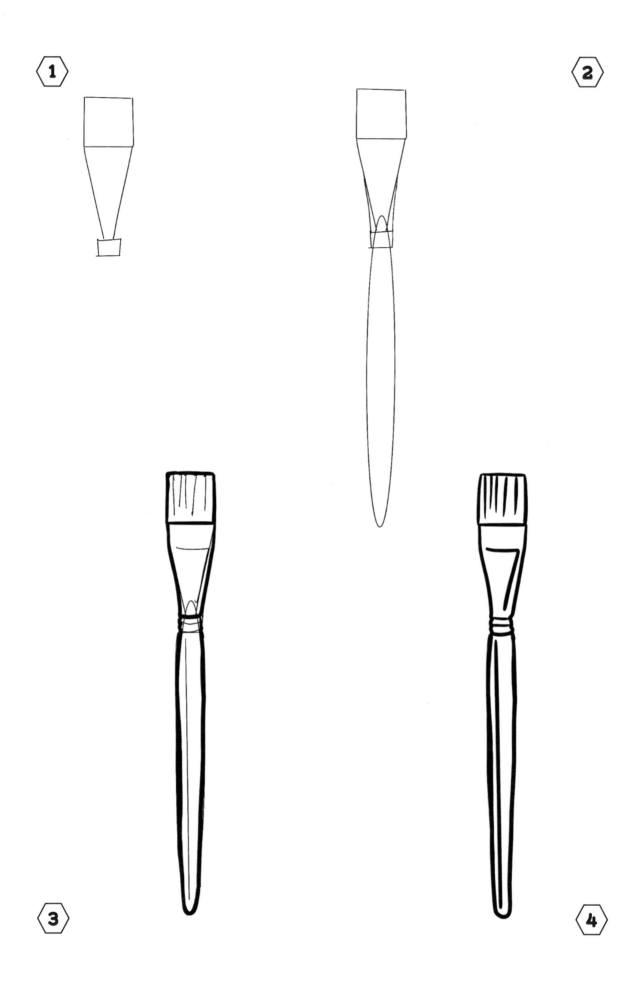

FLIP

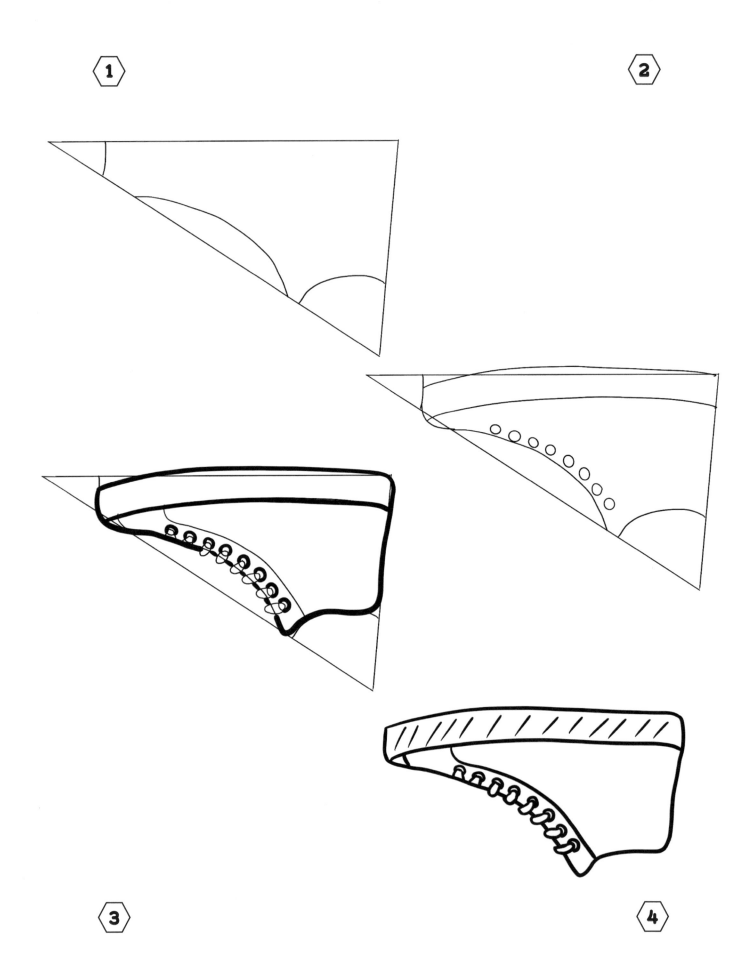

FLIP

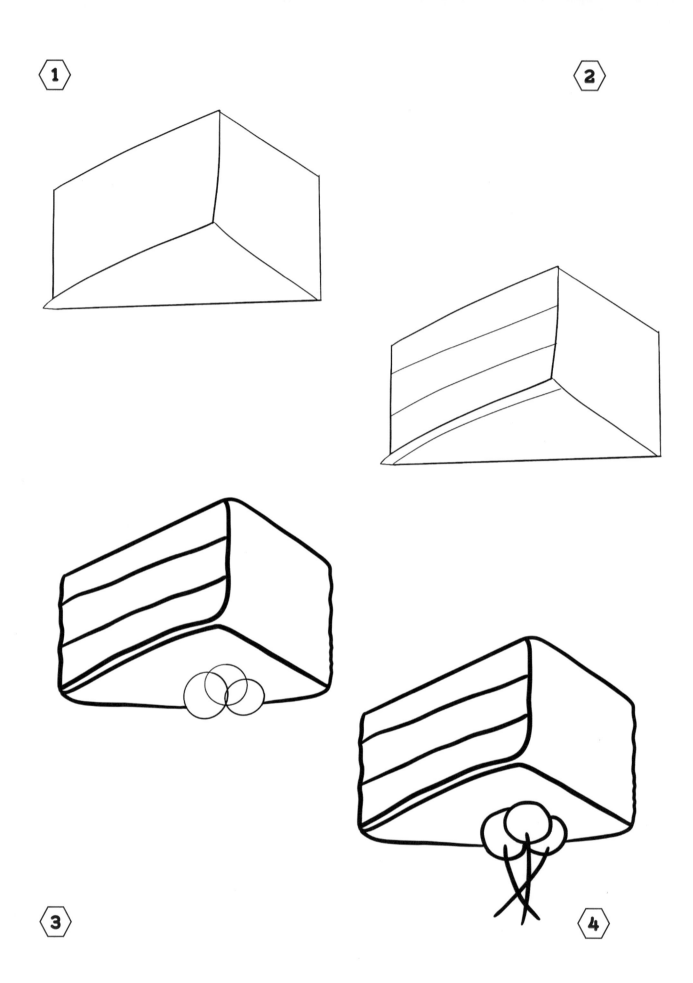

FLIP

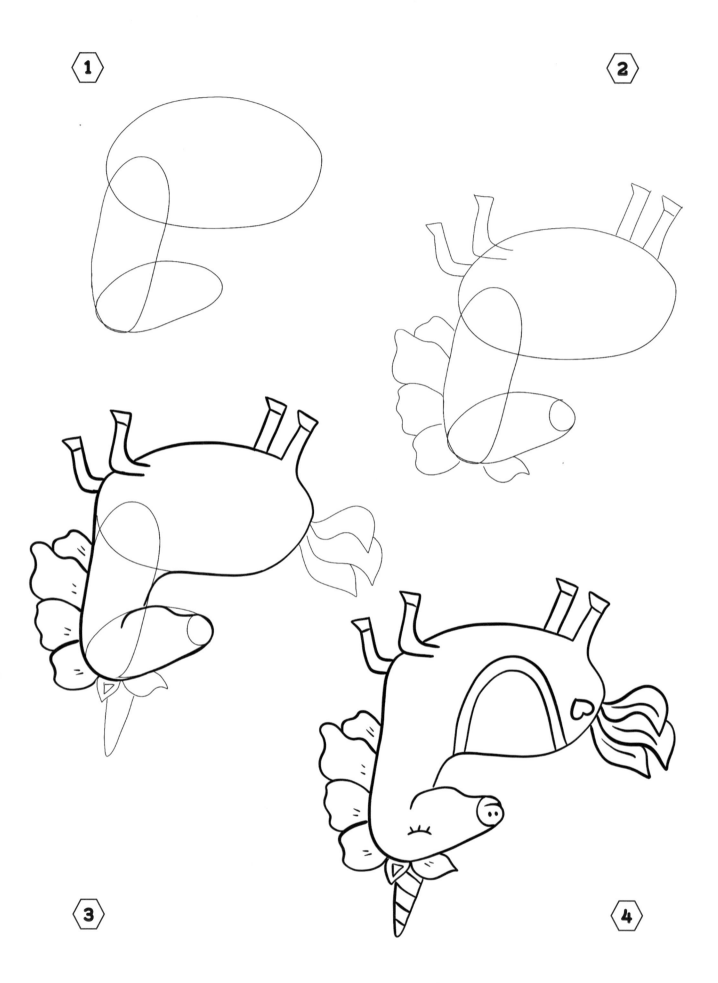

FLIP

FLIP

FLIP

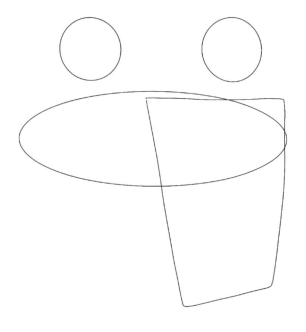
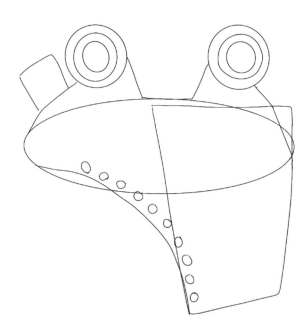
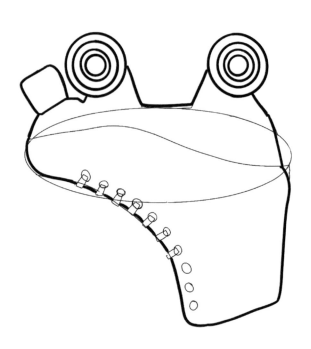
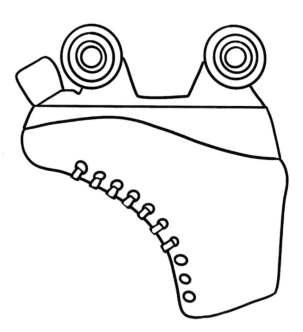

FLIP

FLIP

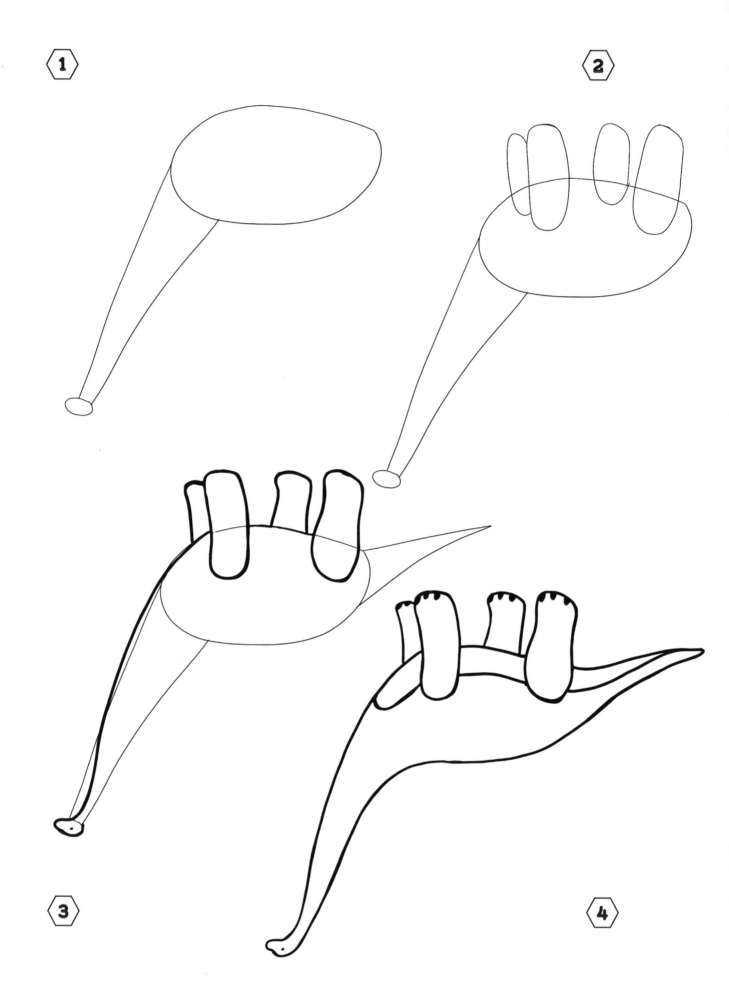

FLIP

FLIP

FLIP

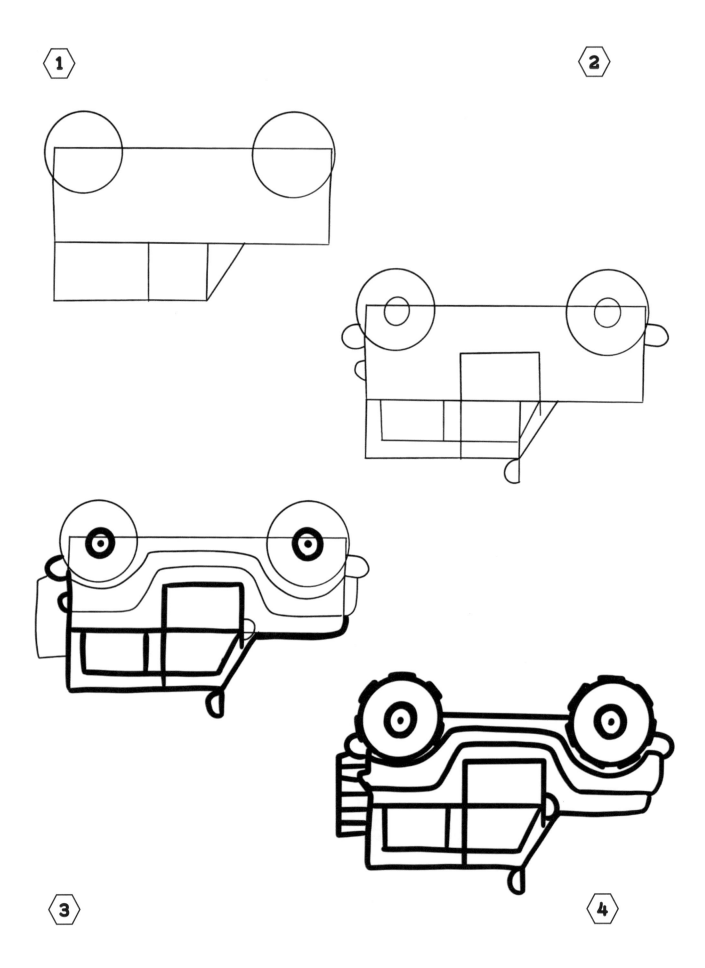

FLIP

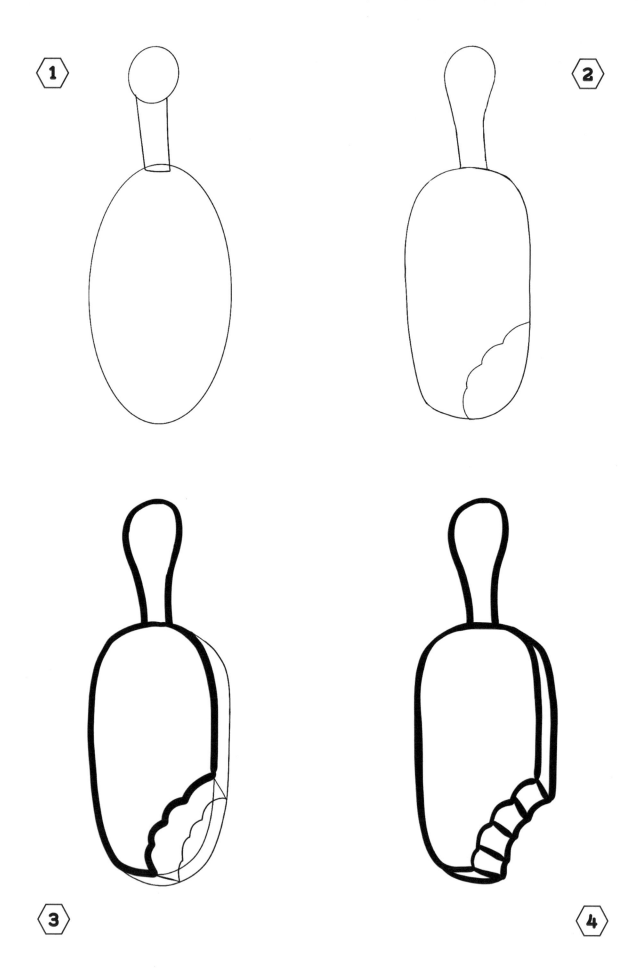

FLIP

FLIP

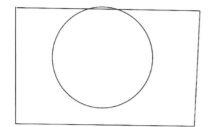

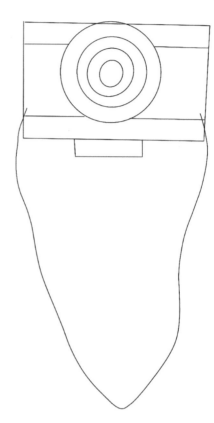
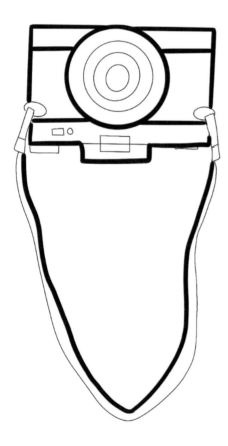
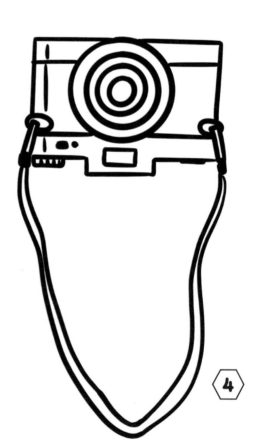

FLIP

FLIP

FLIP

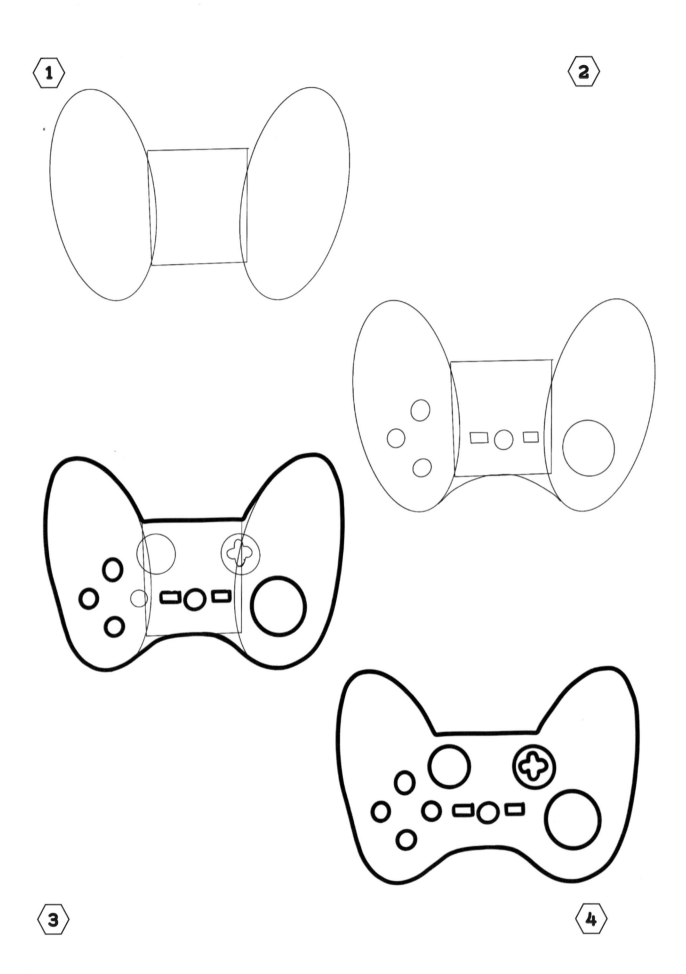

FLIP

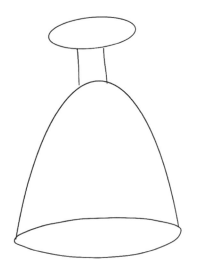
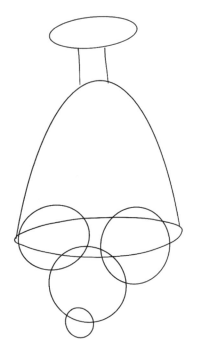
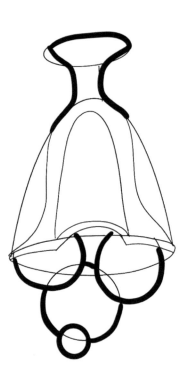
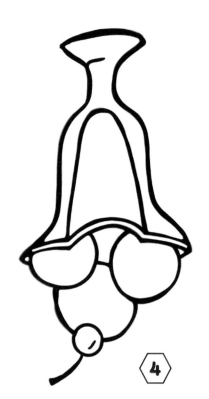

FLIP

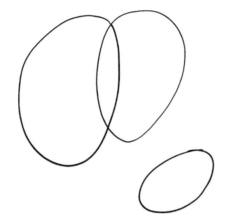

FLIP

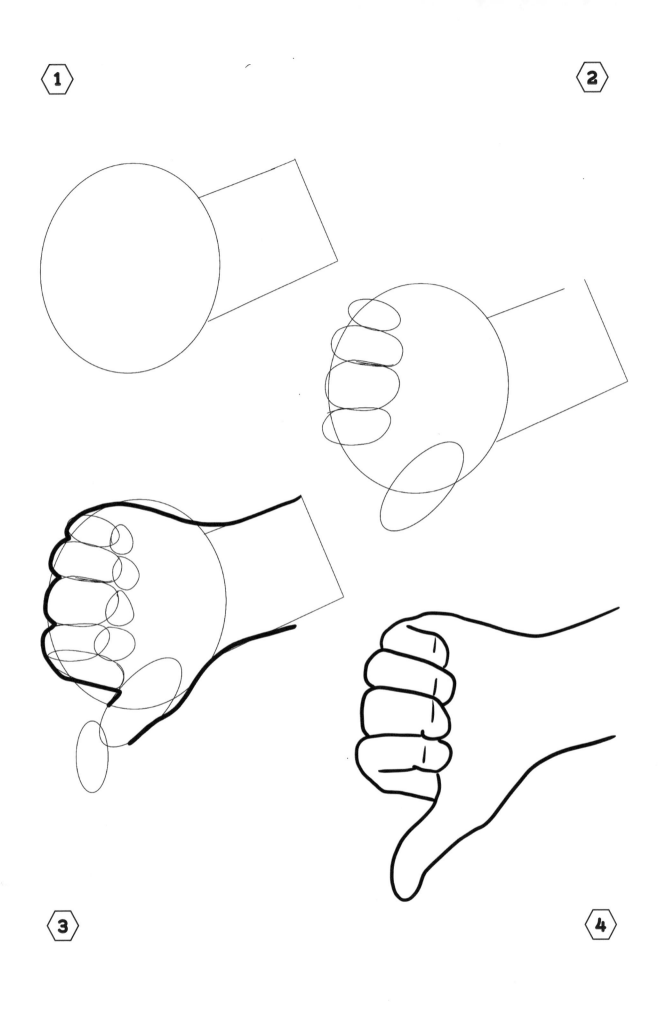

FLIP

FLIP

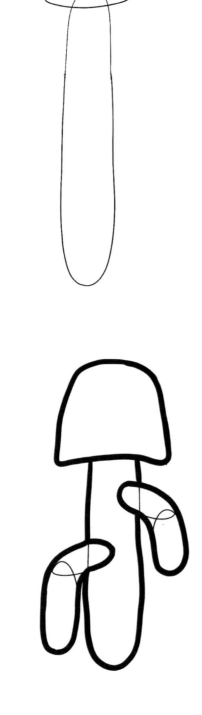

FLIP

1

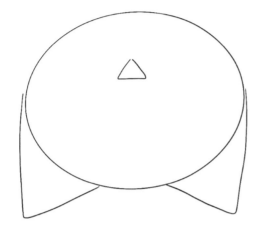

2

3

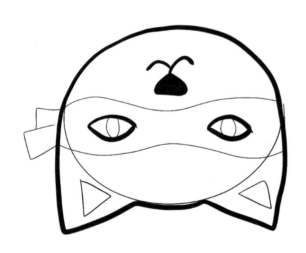

4

FLIP

FLIP

FLIP

FLIP

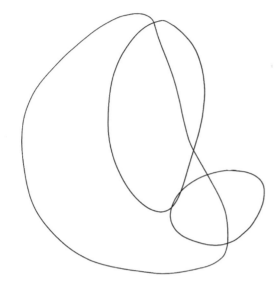
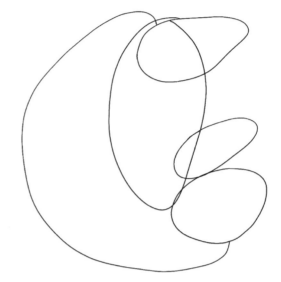
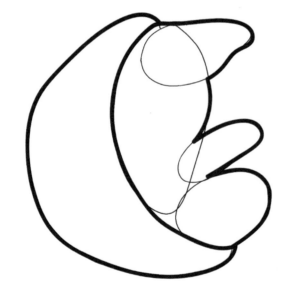

FLIP

FLIP

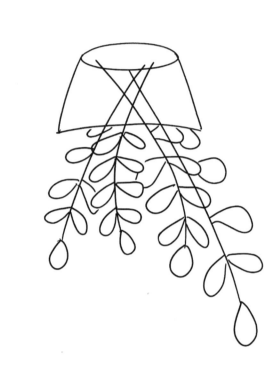

FLIP

FLIP

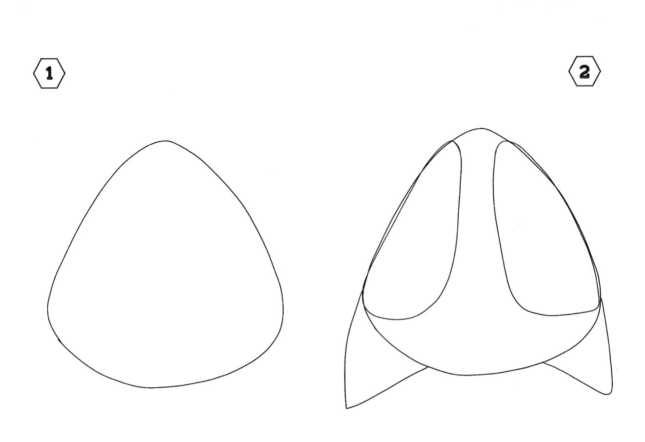
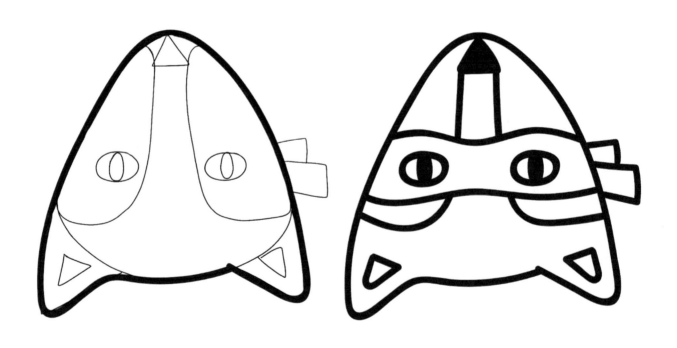

FLIP

① ②

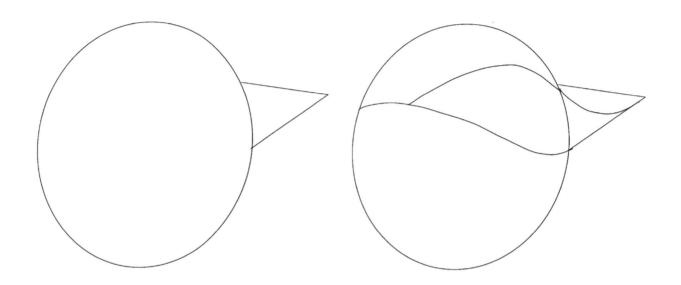

③ ④

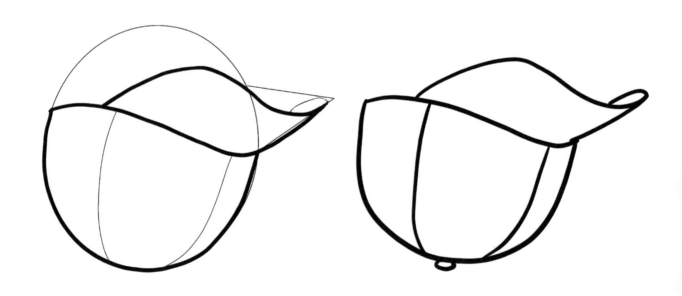

FLIP

FLIP

1

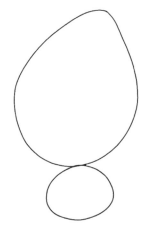

2

3

4

FLIP

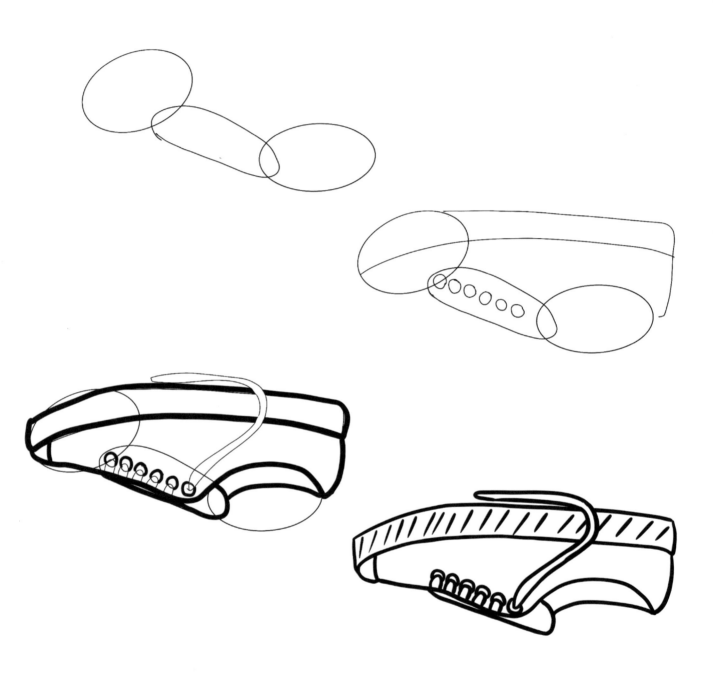

FLIP

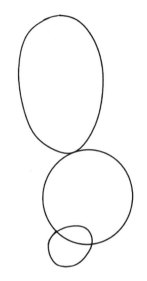
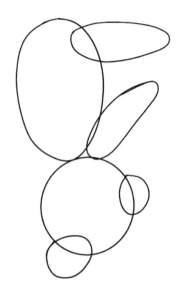
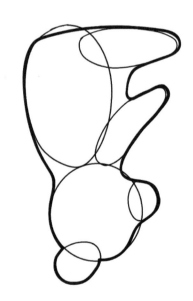
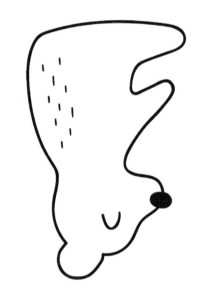

FLIP

FLIP

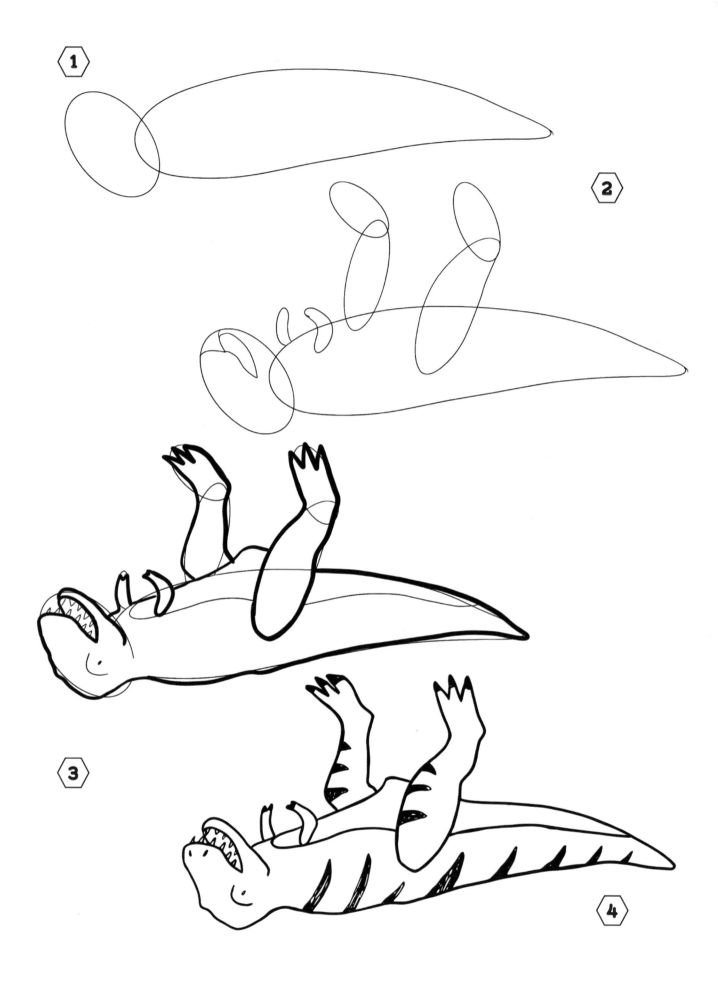

FLIP

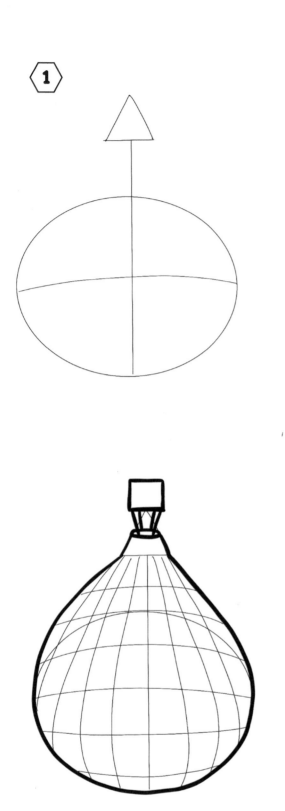
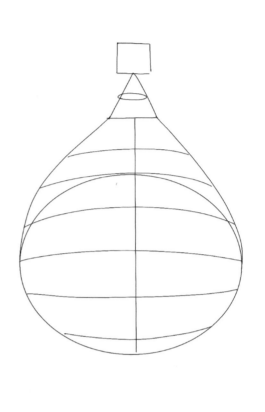

FLIP

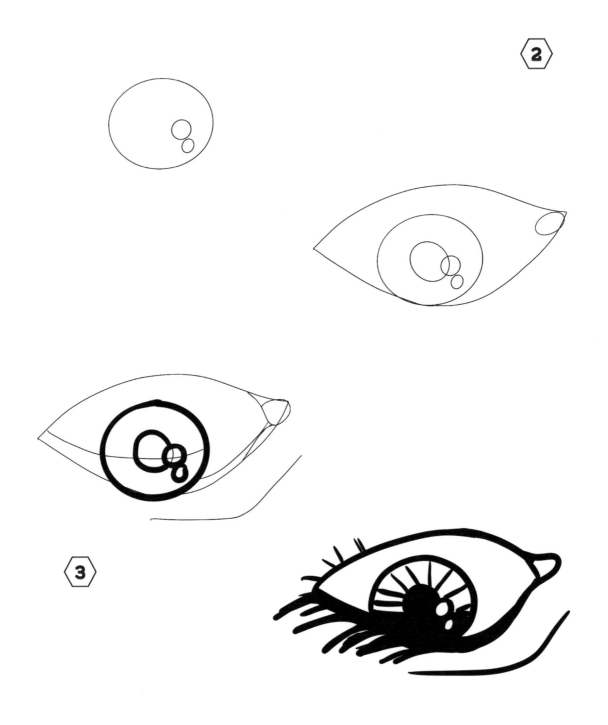

FLIP

FLIP

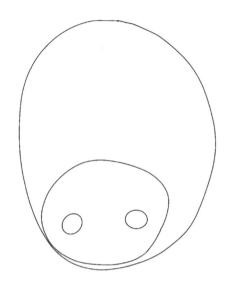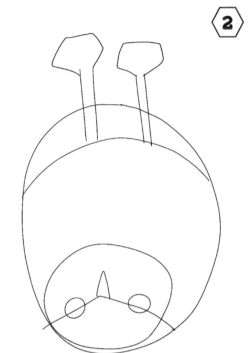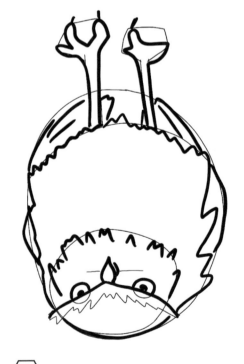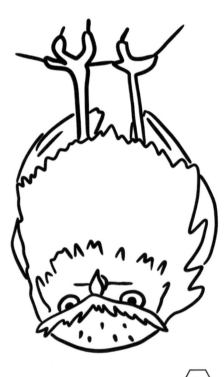

FLIP

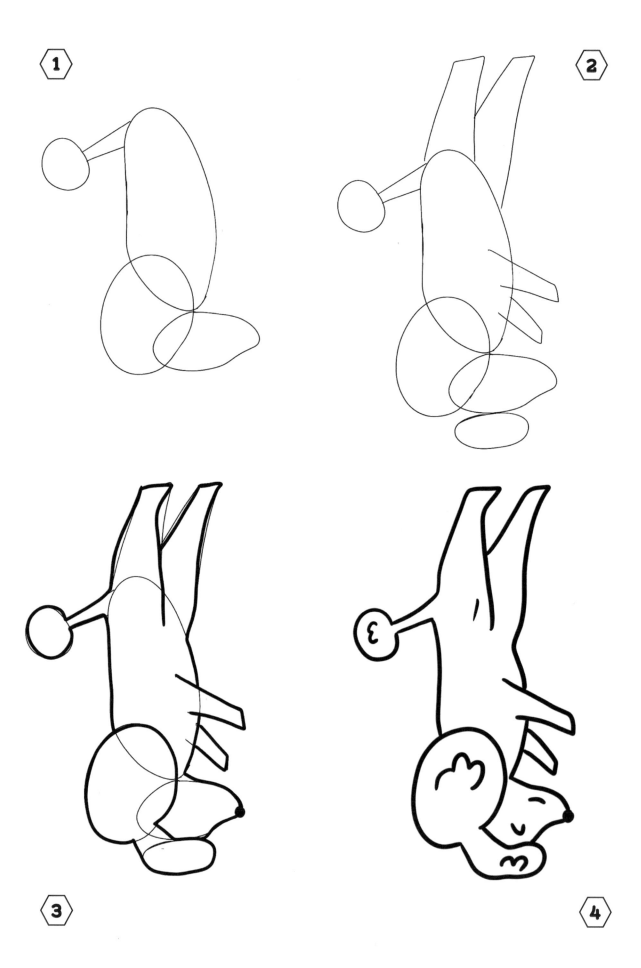

FLIP

FLIP

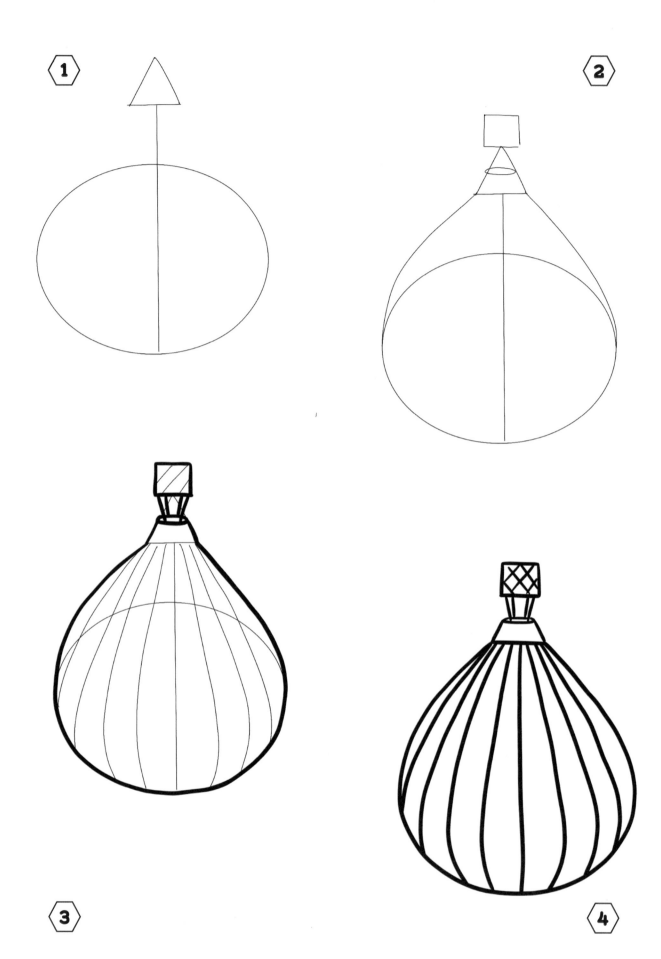

FLIP

FLIP

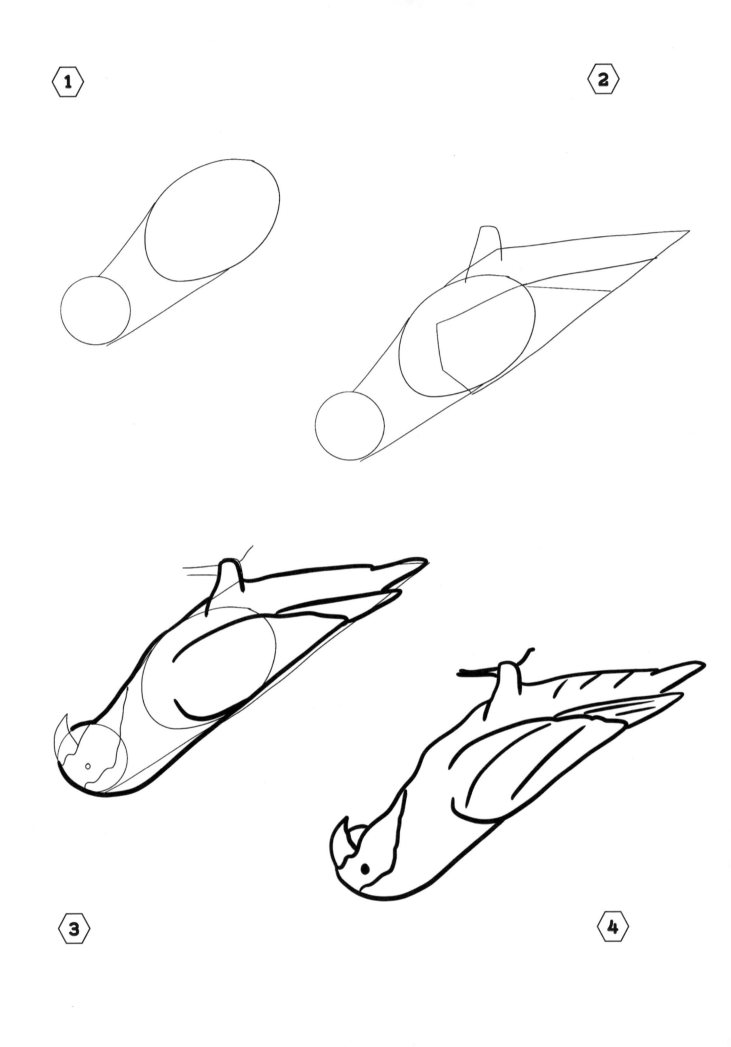

FLIP

FLIP

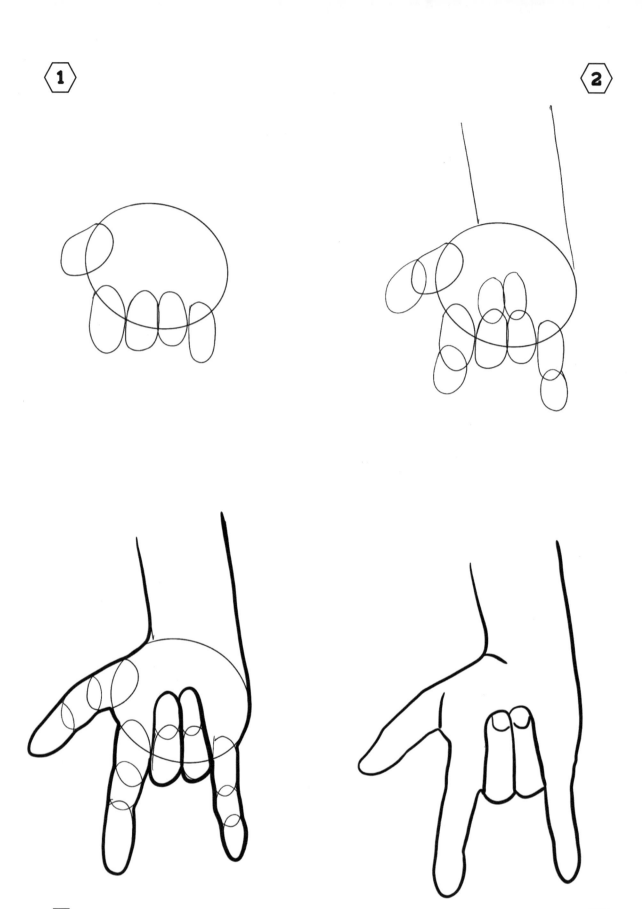

FLIP

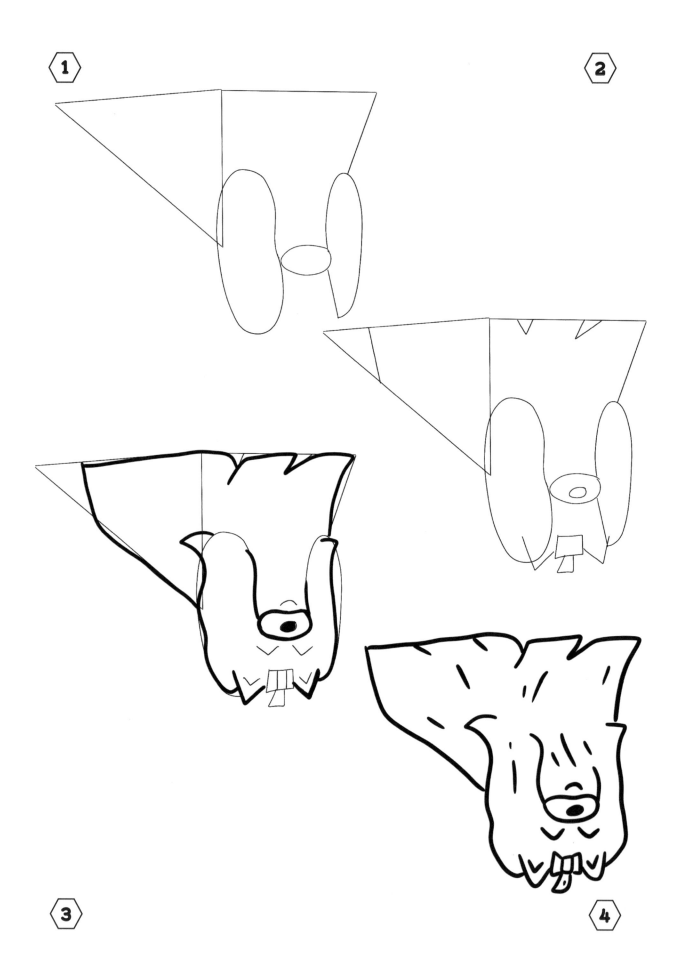

FLIP

FLIP

FLIP

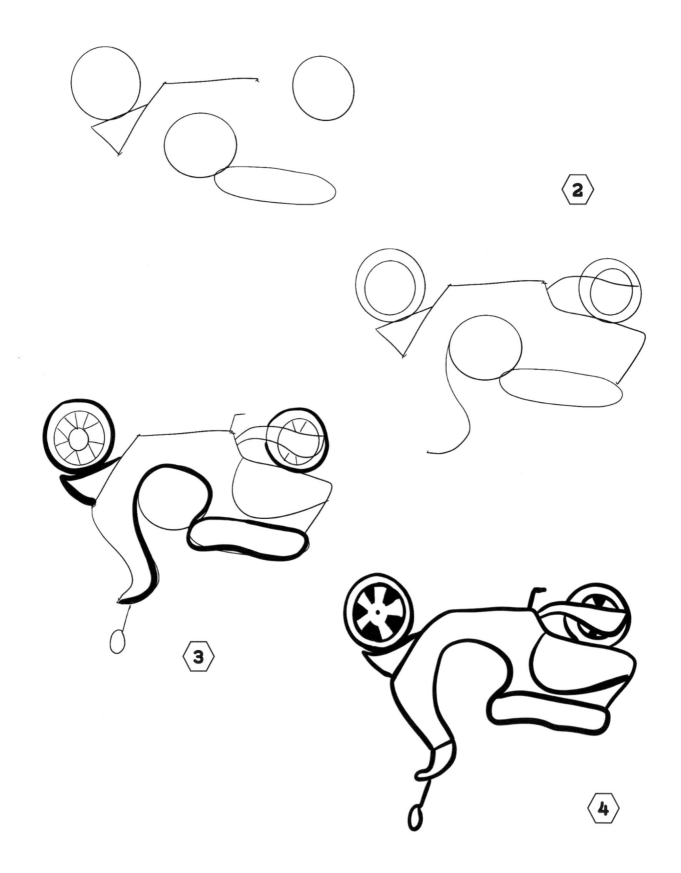

FLIP

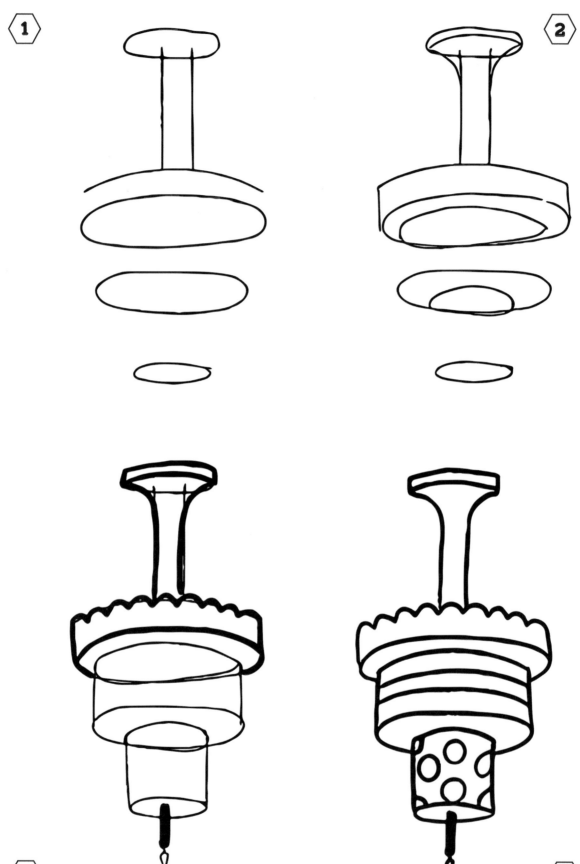

FLIP

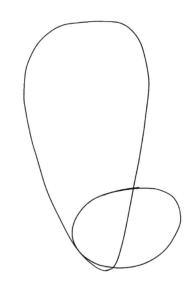

FLIP

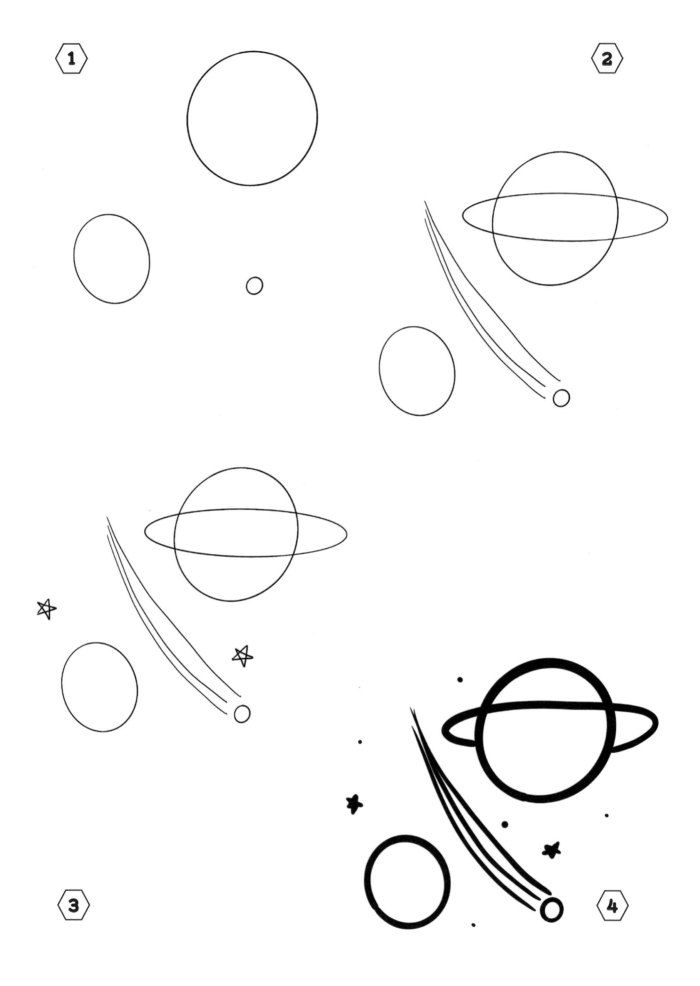

FLIP

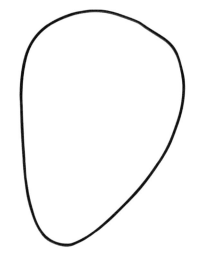
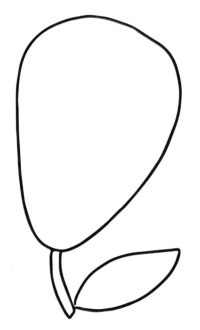

FLIP

1

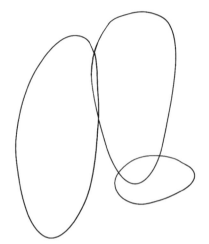

2

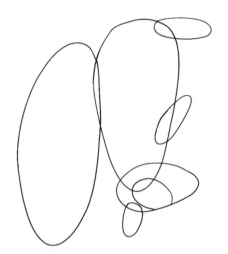

3

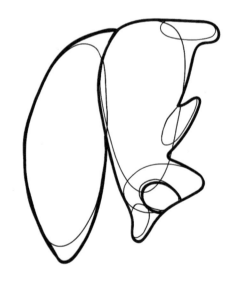

4

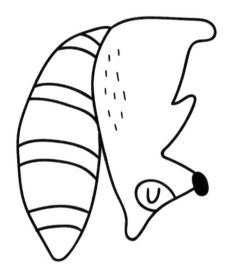

FLIP

FLIP

1

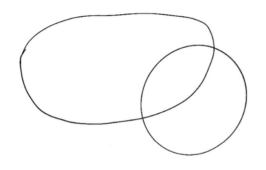

2

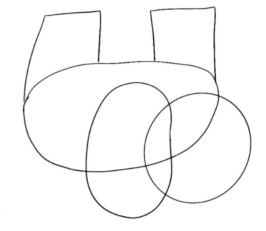

3

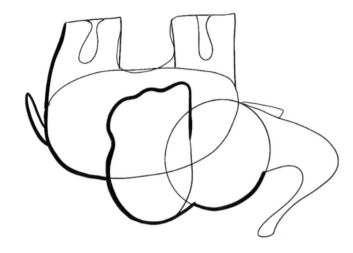

4

FLIP

FLIP

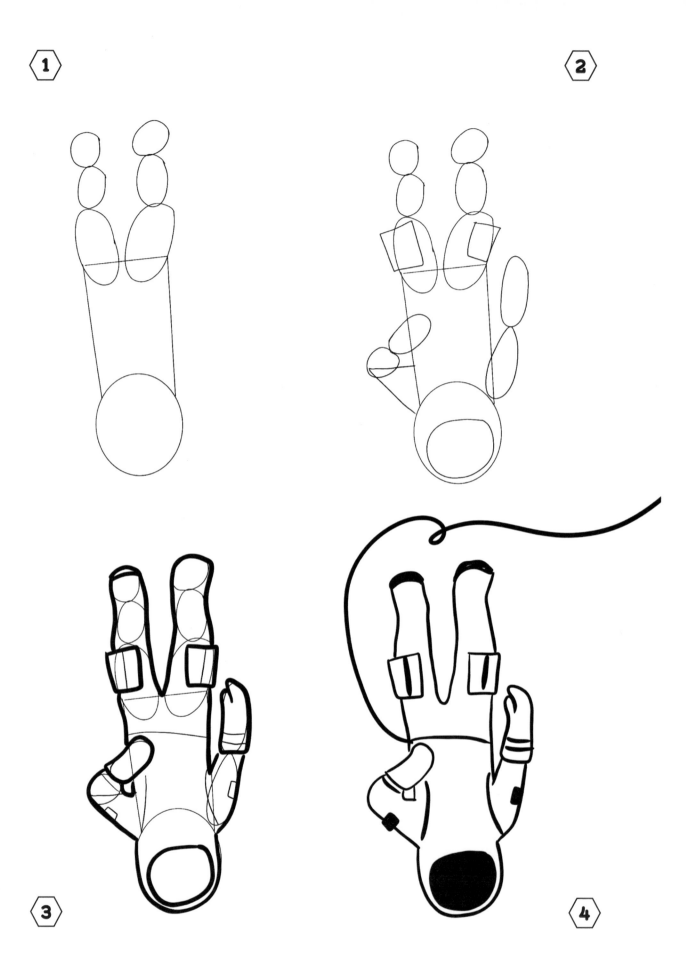

FLIP

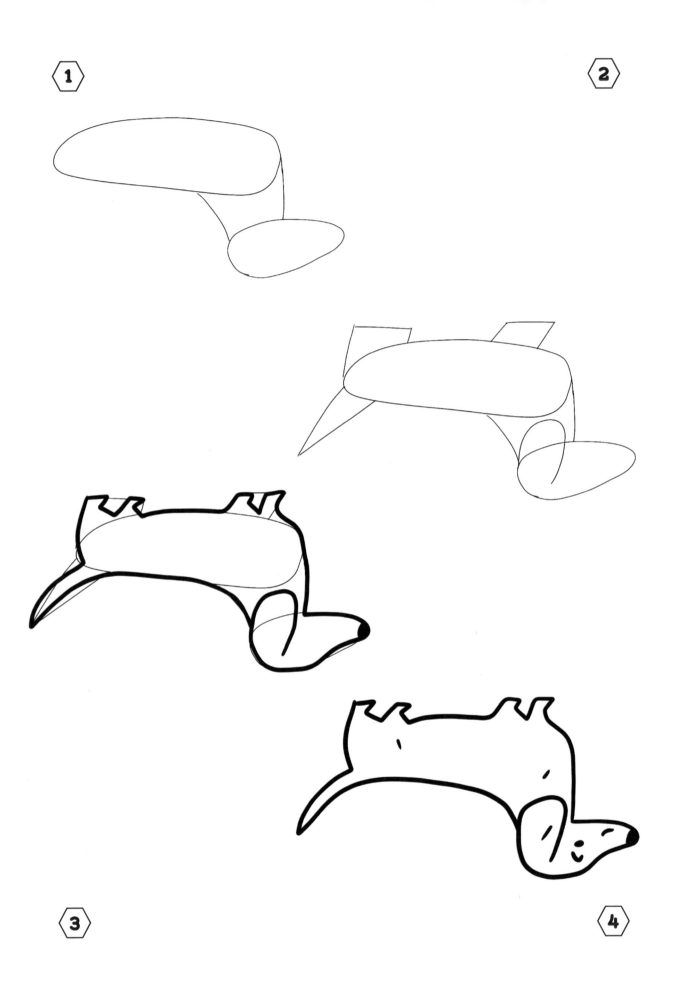

FLIP

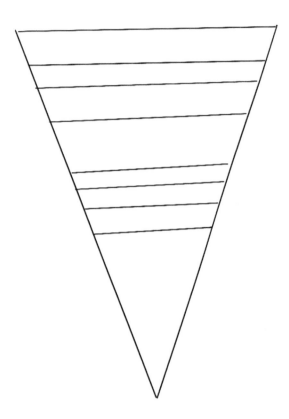
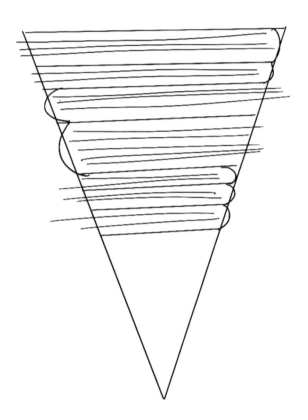

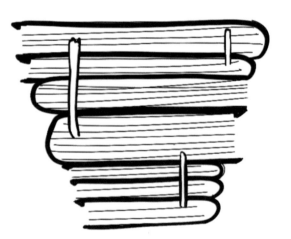

FLIP

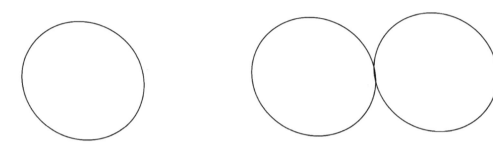
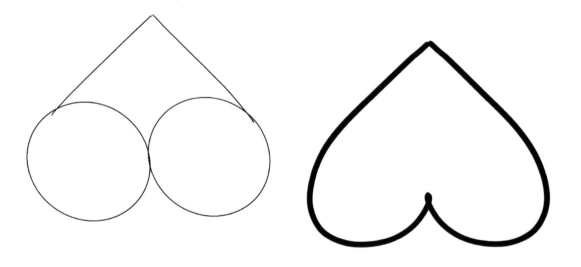

FLIP

FLIP

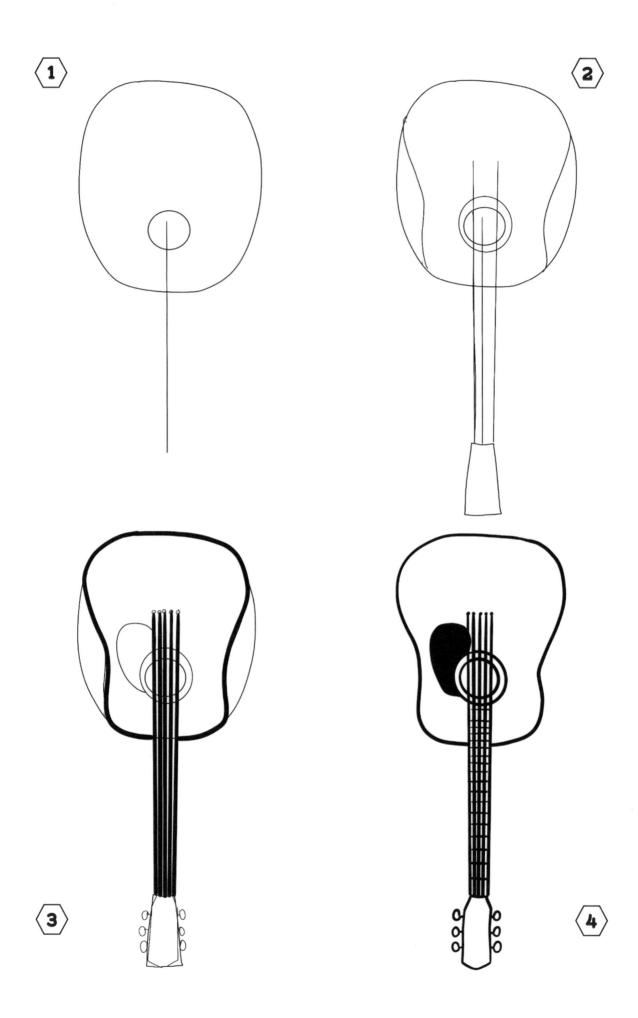

FLIP

FLIP

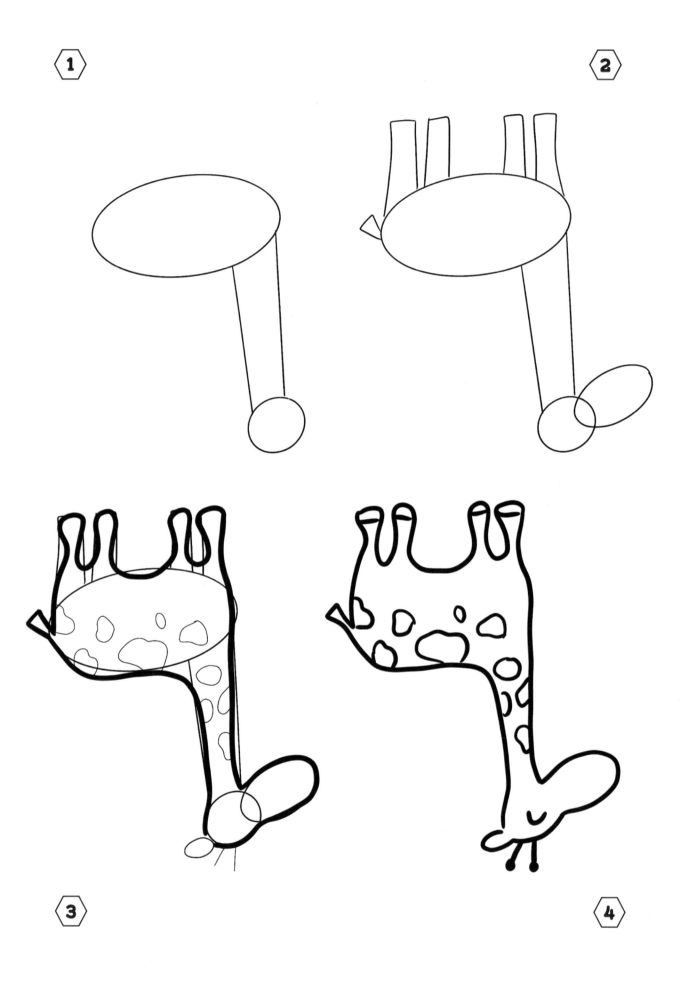

FLIP

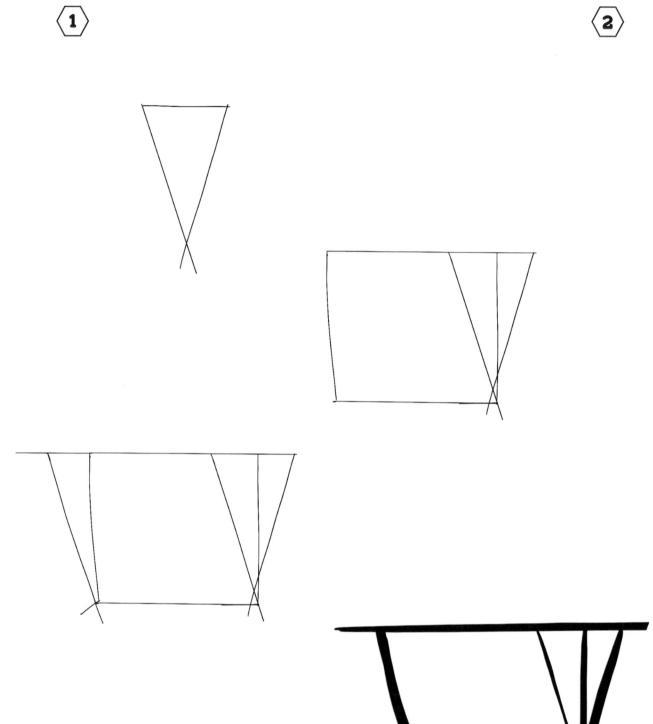

FLIP

FLIP

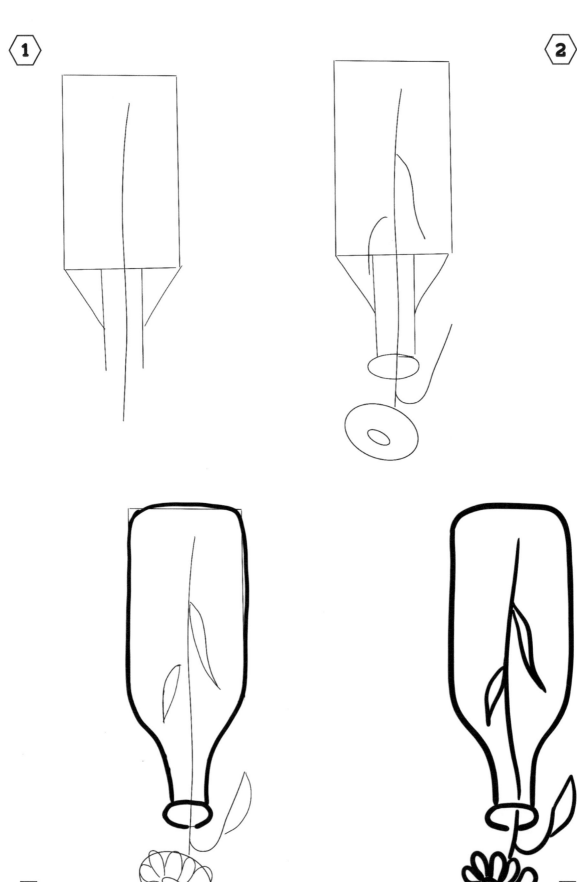

FLIP

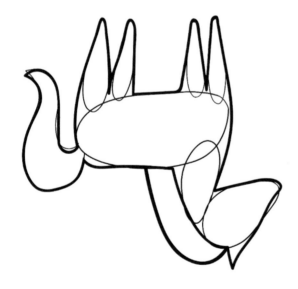

FLIP

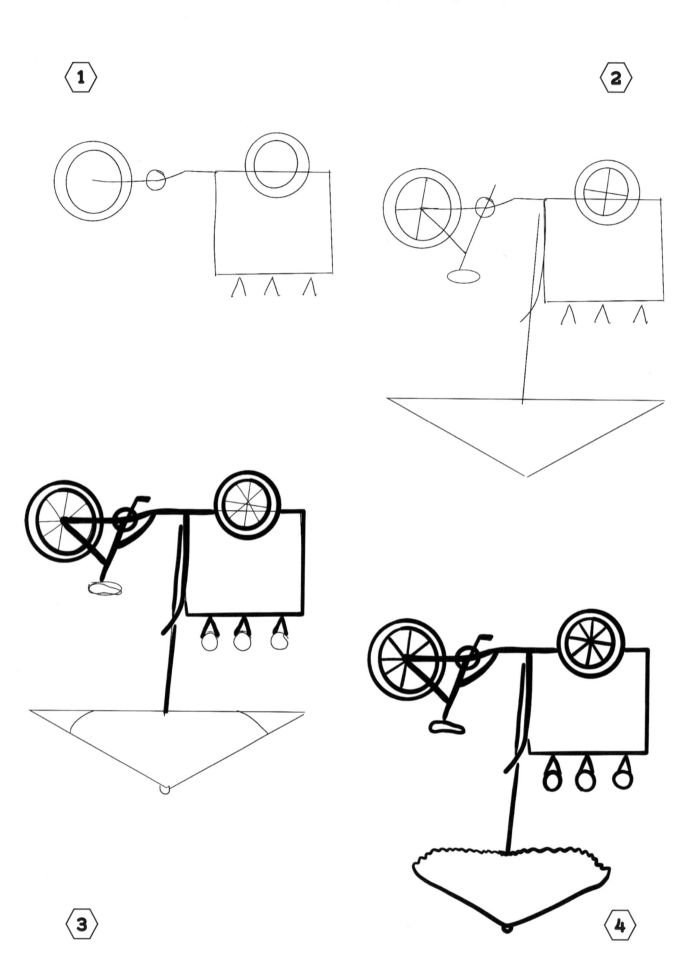

FLIP

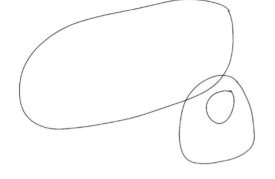
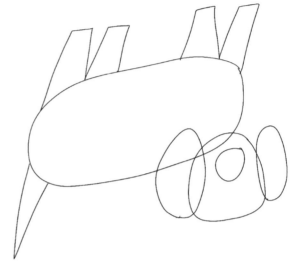
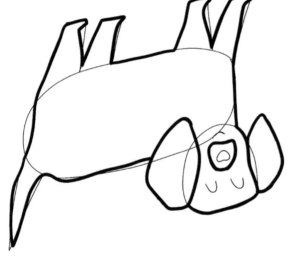

FLIP

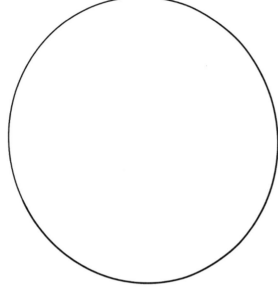
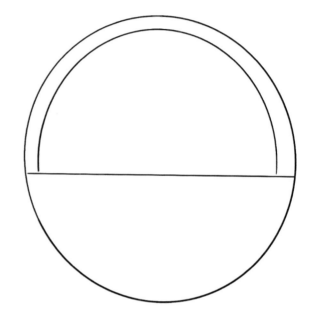
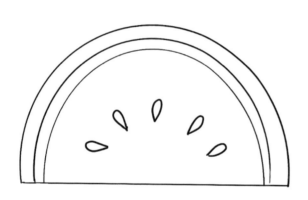

FLIP

FLIP

FLIP

FLIP

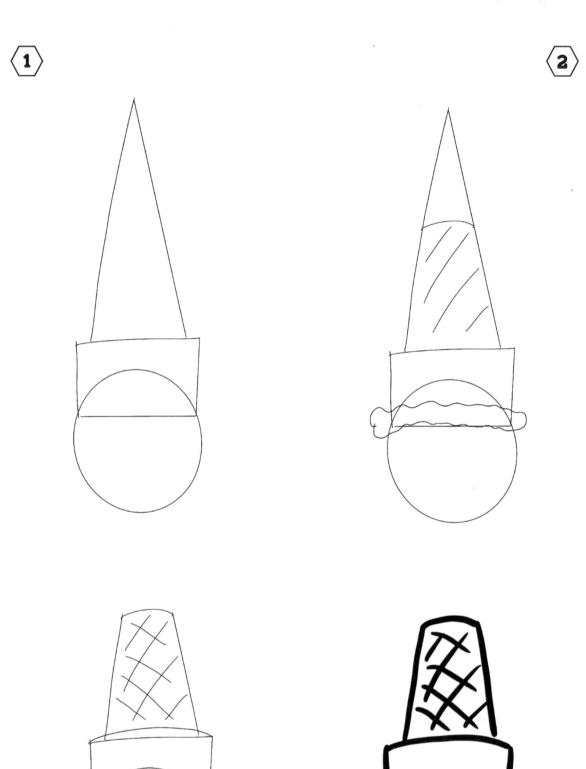

FLIP

FLIP

FLIP

FLIP

1

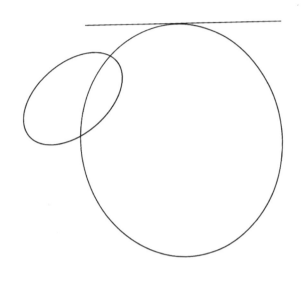

2

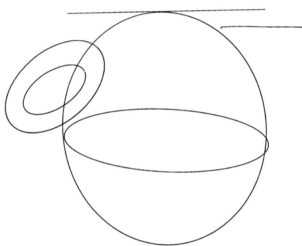

3

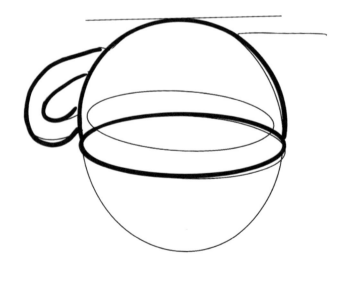

4

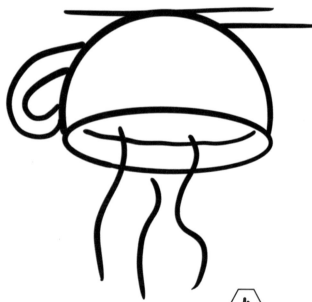

FLIP

FLIP

FLIP

FLIP

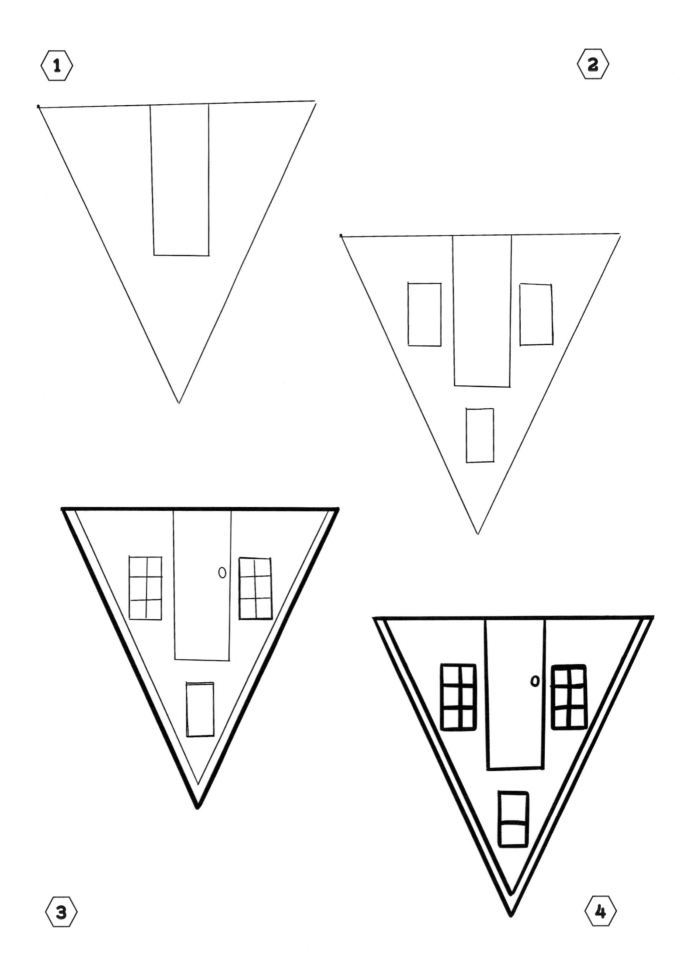

FLIP

①
②
③
④

FLIP

FLIP

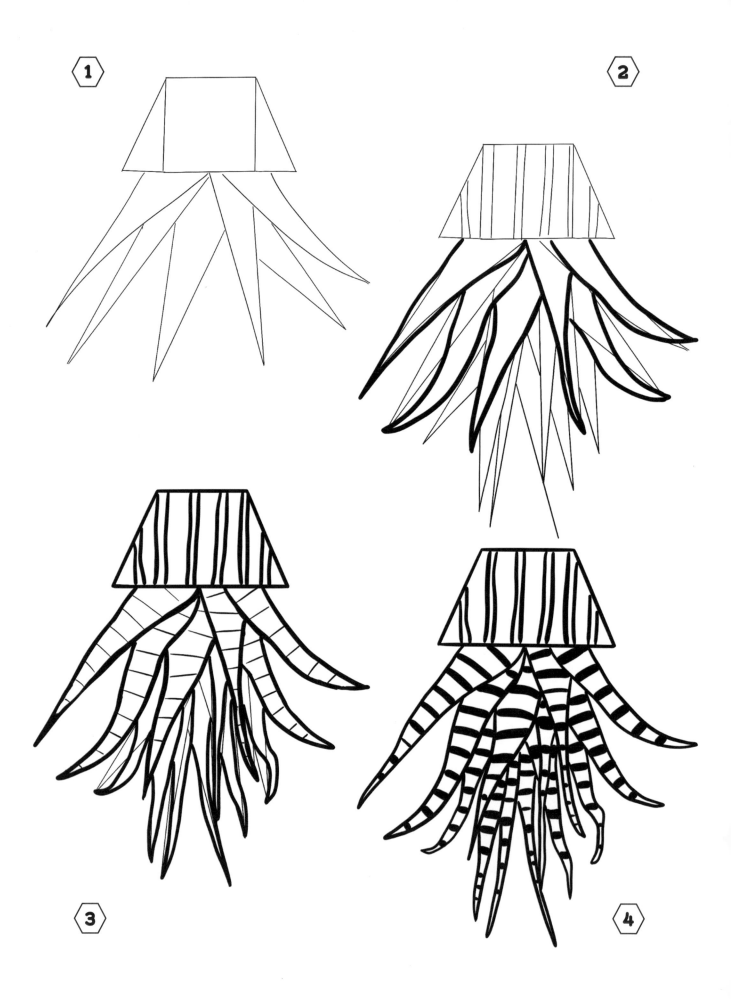

FLIP

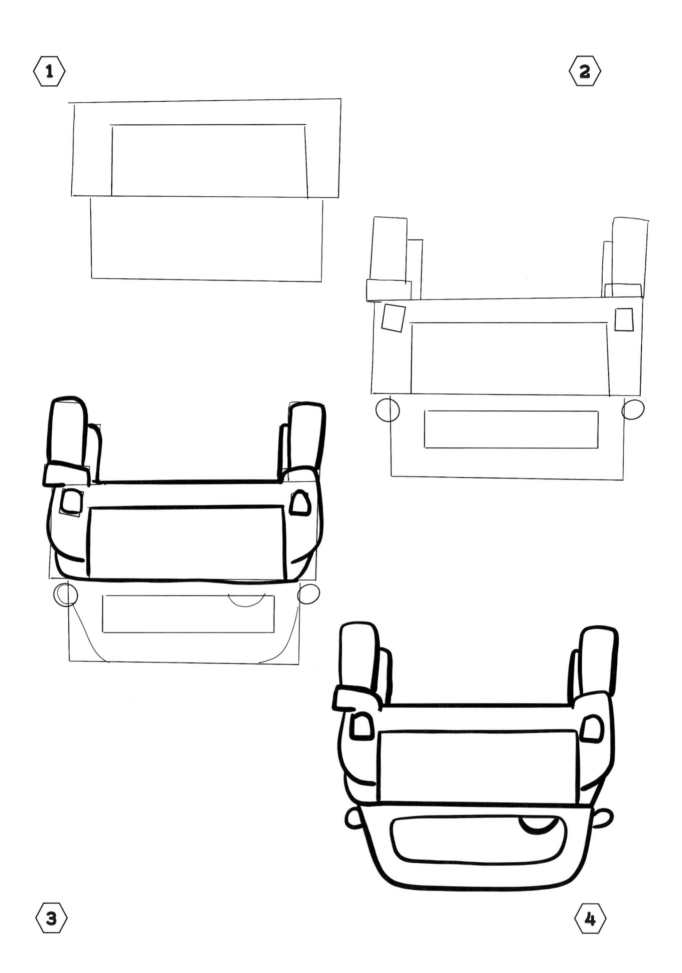

FLIP

FLIP

①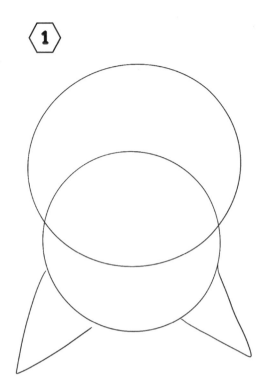
②
③
④

FLIP

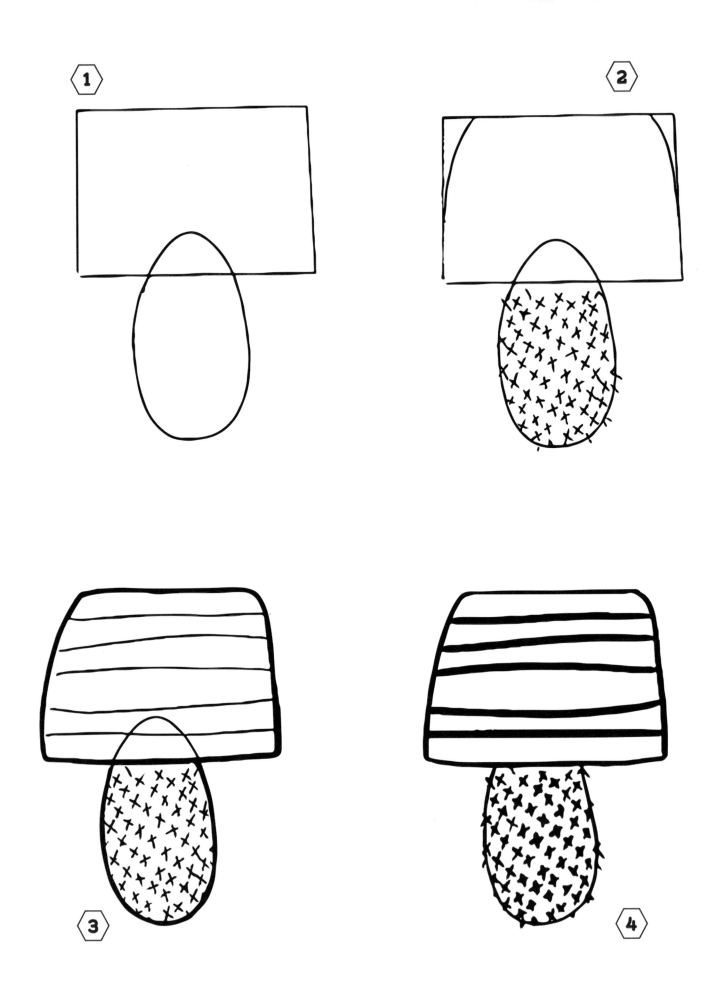

FLIP

FLIP

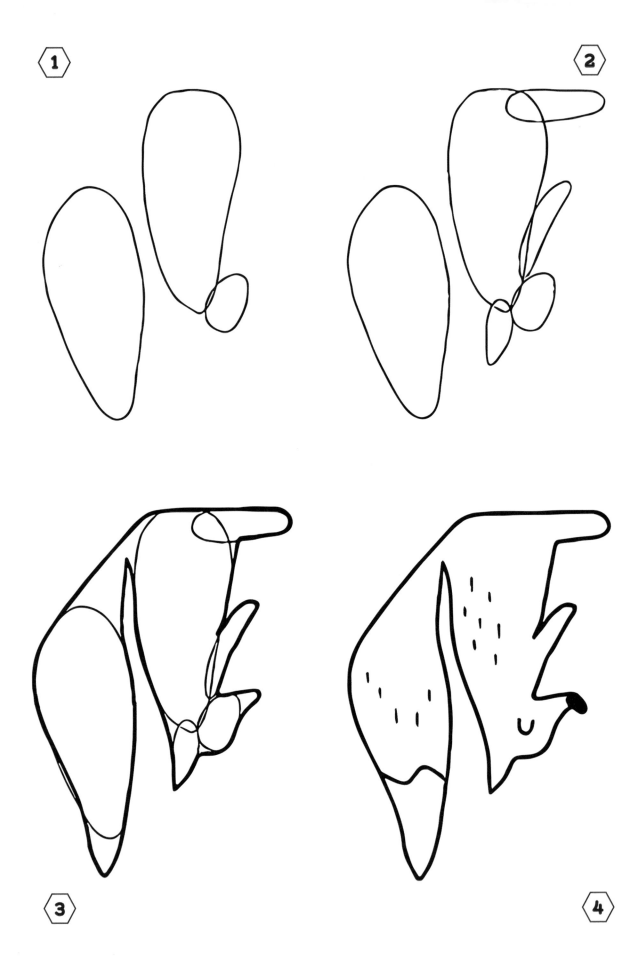

FLIP

FLIP

FLIP

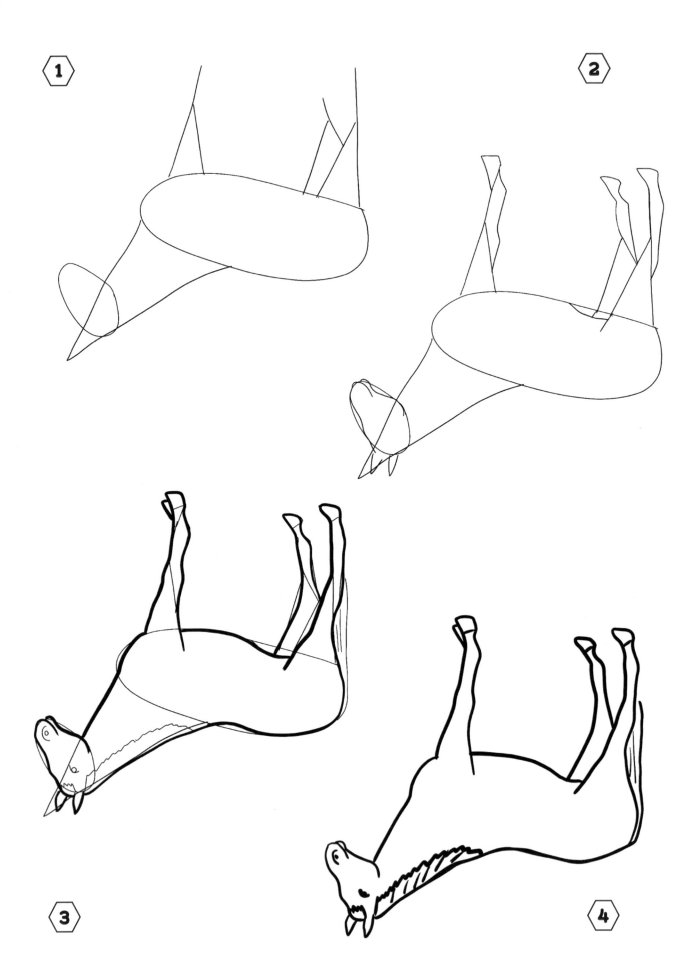

FLIP

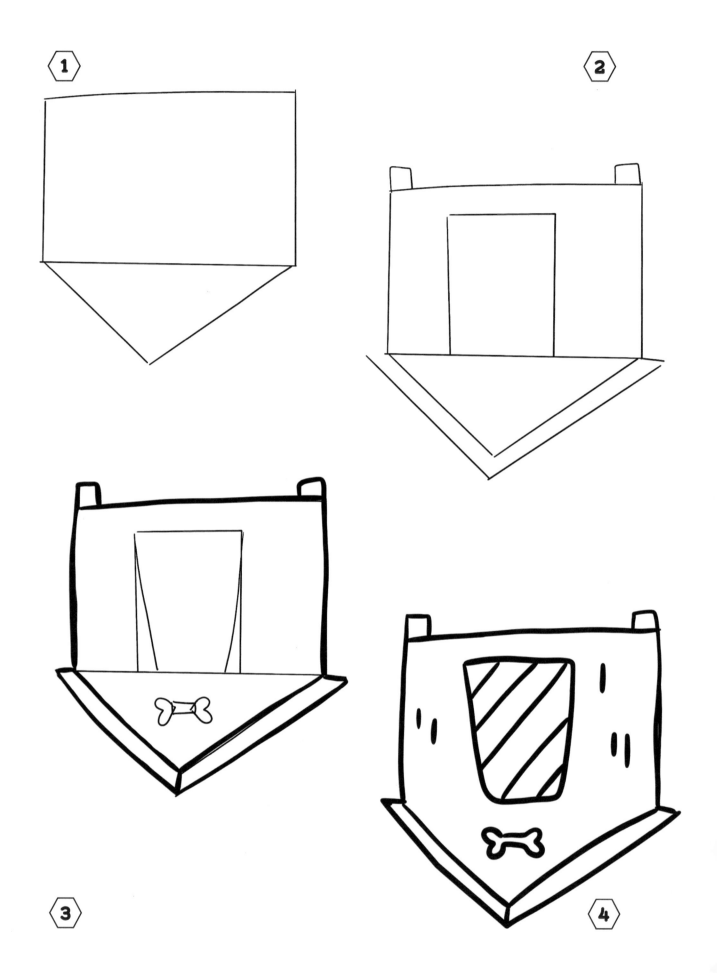

FLIP

FLIP

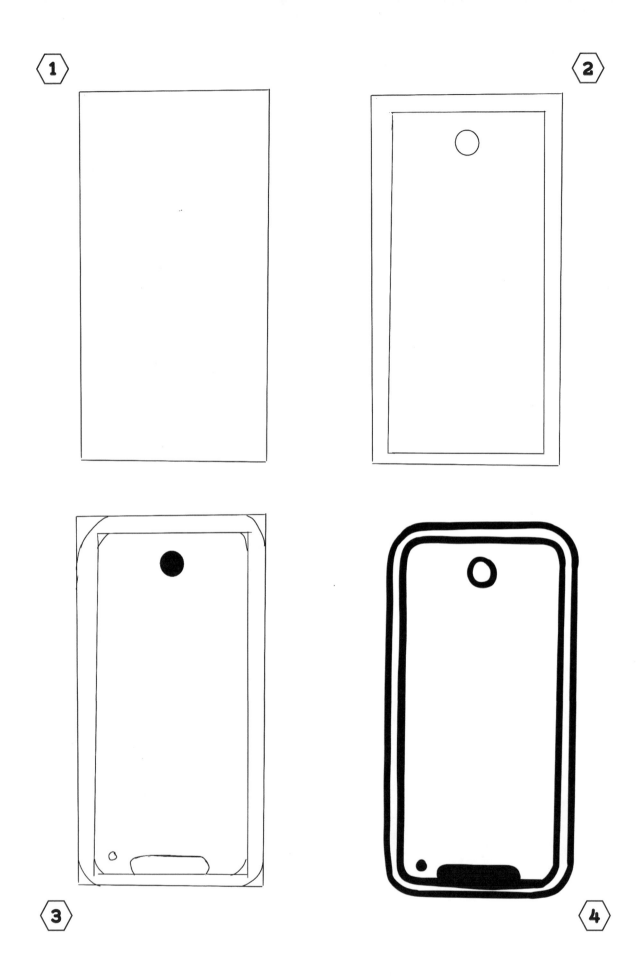

FLIP

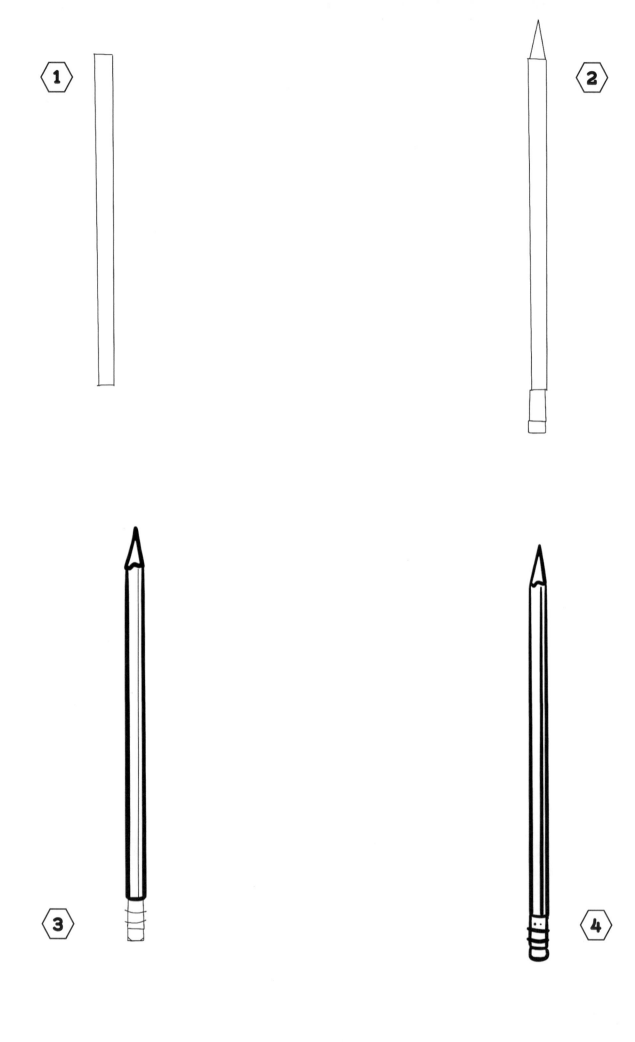

FLIP

FLIP

FLIP

FLIP

FLIP

FLIP

FLIP

FLIP

FLIP

FLIP

FLIP

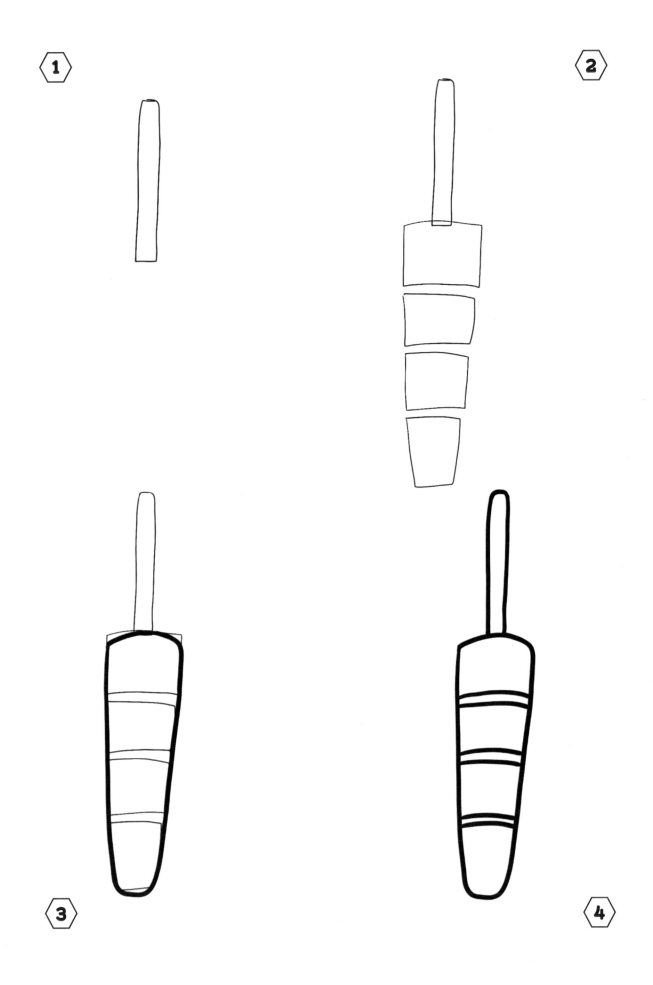

FLIP

FLIP

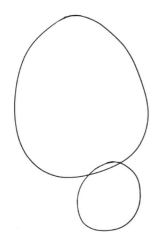

FLIP

FLIP

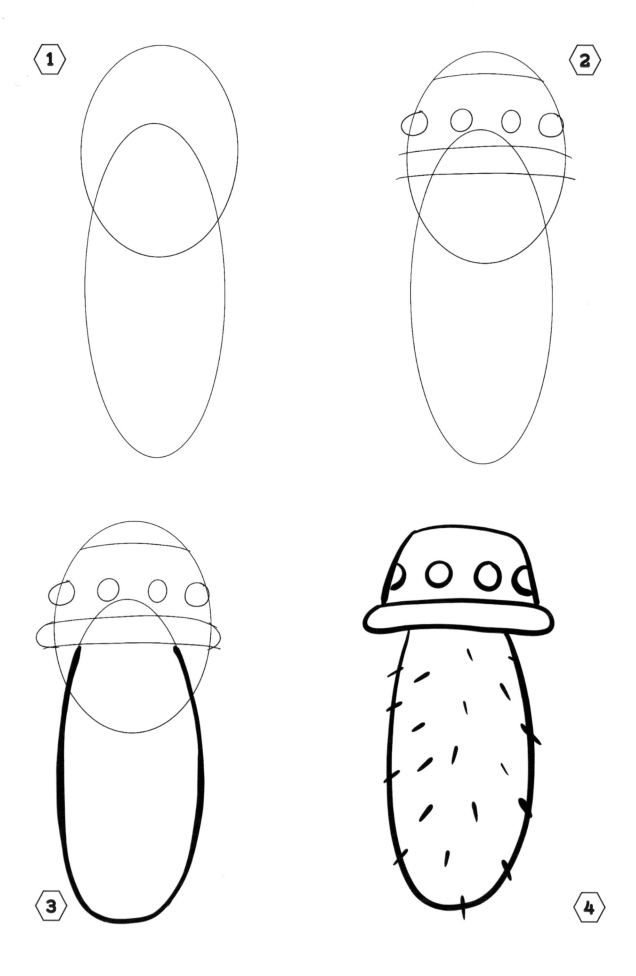

FLIP

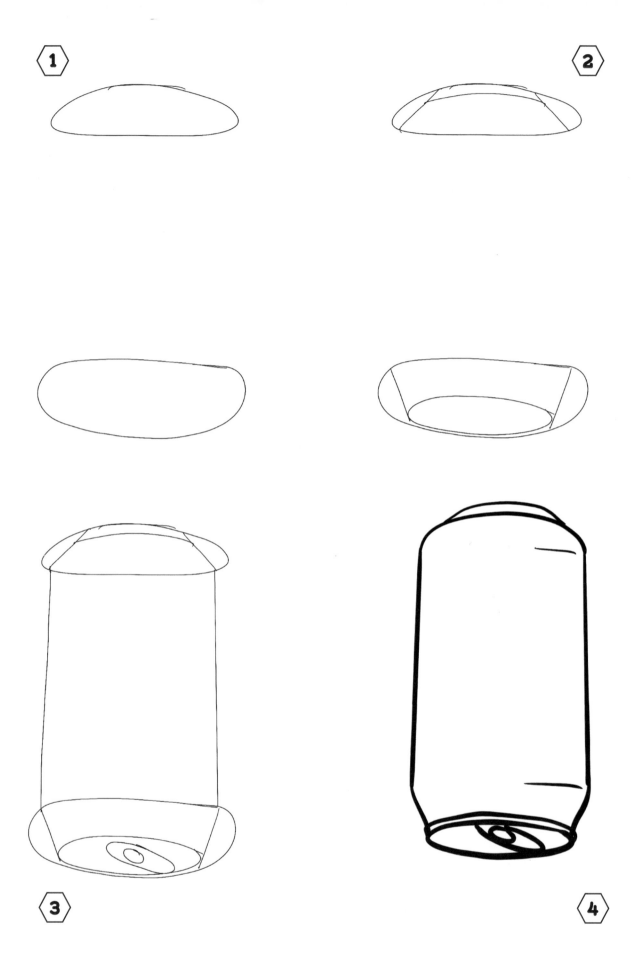

FLIP

FLIP

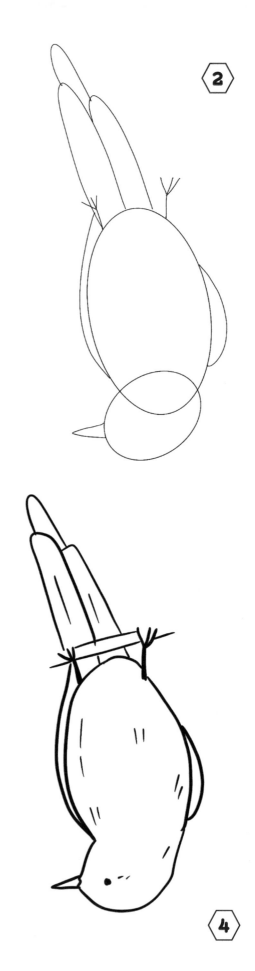

FLIP

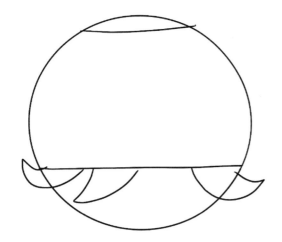

FLIP

FLIP

Made in the USA
Thornton, CO
04/23/23 20:47:11

d49f8e89-54d7-4429-a48a-0a88b48a5be0R01